T H E

{ CHEAP }
Bastard's
G U I D E™

to
San Francisco

Secrets of Living the Good Life—for **FREE!**

Karen Solomon

The
Globe
Pequot
Press

GUILFORD, CONNECTICUT

The prices, rates, and hours listed in this guidebook were confirmed at press time. We recommend, however, that you call establishments to obtain current information before traveling.

To buy books in quantity for corporate use
or incentives, call **(800) 962–0973**
or e-mail **premiums@GlobePequot.com.**

Library of Congress Cataloging in Publication Data is Available.

ISBN: 978-0-7627-4367-4

Manufactured in the United States of America
First Edition/First Printing

To Big Mel, who yelled at us for leaving too much ketchup on our plates.

To the Chumps and the Ladies Auxiliary of Chump, who know
that the value of "free" is pure freedom.

To Aunty Mame, who has shown me, repeatedly,
that freeloaders can live the high life.

And of course, my endless gratitude and love to Matthew and Emmett, who
remind me every single day that the best things in life really are free.

{ CONTENTS }

{ INTRODUCTION }

"If you would be wealthy, think of saving as well as getting."

—Benjamin Franklin

When I moved to San Francisco in 1996, I had the good fortune to arrive just as the wave of dot-coms was beginning to crest. Money was sloshing in every direction, and I quickly landed on my feet with an insanely lucrative writing career and more cash than my post-graduate self knew what to do with (almost all of which is long gone, now that writers' salaries have returned to normal).

What I remember most fondly from that time are the launch parties—the copious, over-the-top, insane displays of wealth to announce the world's arrival of FiveMinutesAgo.com (how *did* we ever live without it?). I saw Devo play for free. I watched pig races on Treasure Island for nothin'. I drank a frat house worth of booze every week and never had to leave the tip. People traded guest list status ("I'll take you to Kaboozle.com's launch on Tuesday if you bring me to iGazoontite.com on Thursday!"). Web sites like SFGirl.com, Oliver's List, and Scrounging.net opened the floodgates to free booze and high-hog living for those like me who were cheap at heart. Never in my life have I supped on so many raw bars, drank so many top-shelf cognacs, or draped myself in so many T-shirts, watches, and other schwag on someone else's dime.

The freeloading heyday came to a quick end. As the party machine rusted and clogged, the festivities became fewer, further between, and less impressive. You know . . . more like a regular party, not a bacchanalian free-for-all. Eventually they went the way of the dodo.

But one thing has remained with me from this second Bay Area gold rush: the ability to find the party and to push my way to the front of the line for the free open bar. This gorgeous and generous city has heaps to offer the fun-loving tightwad if you know where to find it. In a town where the average apartment costs as much as the GNP of some small countries, any amount of savings is welcome. As I sit here in my hand-me-down hoodie and homemade hat, refusing to put on the heat, typing away on my keypad that I found in the street, and looking at the monitor I've had for eight years, I know that I am not alone. I have friends who have roommates in a studio apartment. I've seen more than one MUNI passenger flash a bus transfer with a thumb over the time. And I have waited in line with hundreds of other bargain hunters for theater tickets, museum entries, and free film screenings just because *we can.* There's a tremendous satisfaction in beating the herd, feeling as if you're getting something for nothing. I am a firm believer in patching, reusing, and making do. If the American economy depended on people like me, we'd rank as high as Greenland on a global financial scale.

The knowledge I have accrued dyeing my own hair and in decades of scouring thrift shops has paid off in the form of this book. I am the self-proclaimed queen of the giveaway, the free trial, the sample, and the discount. My nose has been known to twitch when a "street score" yields a new bookshelf, a set of drinking glasses, or someone else's discarded knitting supplies. My friends and family think that I'm cheap because I just don't see the point in paying full price, but little do they know that I am more than that. I am a Cheap Bastard. Oh, the pennies I have pinched.

In no way does this book take advantage of anyone offering anything that she can't afford to lose. I do not advocate theft, mau-mauing, begging, or persuasion toward the acquisition of free or low-cost goods or services. I have avoided resources solely set aside to help those with low incomes, those who are disabled, the disadvantaged, or the elderly. Every resource listed, unless otherwise noted, is located in San Francisco proper and available to the public at large. Most freebies listed here are events and items that your tax dollars or philanthropic donations have already paid for. A few are free trials and tastes dispensed in the hopes that you'll come back and pay for more. Many are free just because students need practice, such as those who study massage or the culinary arts. Some things are free with a catch—which I disclose. Still other listings in this book are for things that are ridiculously cheap or such a bargain that you'd want to know about them. Cheap Bastards appreciate that sometimes to get a true value, you must part with a little green.

Being a tightwad is a revolutionary act. Kicking our own Gucci butt down a few rungs is a way to remember that the things that are really important in this world are ripe and available for the plucking by anyone, regardless of how much cash lines his purse. In these pages are great tips for things like free babysitting and no-cost tap dancing classes, and for sources of free house paint. But what's in between these frivolities is a manifesto of what it means to live free of the shackles of a thing-driven society. More money may make us happy short term. But taking the time to appreciate all that is offered to us, which may result in losing less cash, is a long-term method of striving toward bliss.

I've learned a lot doing the research for this guide. I am even more in love with San Francisco's kindness and generosity, because its depths are deeper than I'd imagined. The kindest words that you could offer this tome is that you feel you've gotten your money's worth. From one Cheap Bastard to another, I can appreciate what a compliment that truly is.

Karen Solomon

{ SECTION 1:
ENTERTAINMENT
IN SAN FRANCISCO }

{ FILM: }
CHEAP SHOTS

"Hollywood money isn't money.
It's congealed snow, melts in your
hand, and there you are."

—Dorothy Parker

Cheap is good, and free is better, and never is this more true than in the pursuit of entertainment. Those Hollywood fat cats are on notice: We spendthrifts are mad as hell, and we're not going to pay $10 to watch overrated Scientologists strut around on the silver screen anymore! Instead we are digging our hands deeper into our pockets, and digging deeper into the pockets of the Bay Area that believe in the pursuit of cinematic happiness for a lot less dough. Cultural institutes, churches, parks, bars—and sometimes, even movie theaters—are all on board for a tight-fisted traipse in the dark. Close your eyes, and what do you see? The movies for less than most suckers pay. Sit back and enjoy the show.

Artists' Television Access

992 Valencia
(415) 824-3890
www.atasite.org

From the heart of the Mission, this tiny, bedraggled space has packed a real punch since it first took root in the community in 1984. Today this madam is showing her age, but she is still an indispensable asset for young filmmakers (and visual artists and sometimes even musicians) to showcase their wares in an intimate and welcoming setting that would never fly in the mainstream. Expect cutting-edge artistic vision, nonnarrative explorations of the human psyche, documentaries galore, and stuff that's just plain dumbfounding—er, OK, "groundbreaking." Check the Web site for the film schedule.

THE CATCH
Most screenings are $5 to $6.

Bernal Heights Outdoor Cinema

Various locations in Bernal Heights
www.bhoutdoorcine.org

September and October

This neighborhood film event features terrific shorts from local filmmakers, many of which showcase the city itself. These are often family affairs; picnics, minus the booze, are welcome. Add your name to the mailing list to learn about next season's offerings.

CHEAT THE CHAINS

Numerous theaters in San Francisco and the Bay Area, including the Embarcadero Cinema, Opera Plaza, the Bridge, the Clay, and the Lumiere, are owned under the national Landmark Theaters umbrella. There's not much one can do to avoid the $10 ticket price (heck, even the "bargain" matinees and kids' seats are still eight bucks), but they do offer a poorly publicized bargaining tool. Multiple ticket cards can be purchased at the box office only. A book of five passes sells for $38.00 (about $7.25 per ticket), but all passes must be used within six months, and they cannot be used for shows on Friday and Saturday after 6:00 P.M. Celluloid-loving cheapskates with money to spend will want to take advantage of a book of 25 passes for $175 ($7 per ticket), which never expire and can be used anytime. Better yet, sign up to learn about occasional free screenings at www.landmarktheatres.com/MailBag/FilmClubIndex_frameset.htm.

CELLspace
2050 Bryant Street
(415) 648-7562
www.cellspace.org/events

Versatile and multimedia-centric, there is always something cinematic happening here in between the visual arts and performance, though it's more likely to be DVD than celluloid. The "media arts cluster" offers low-cost video editing space and other film-related classes and workspace, thus attracting the DIY moviemaking crowd. Low-priced screening fees mean the savings are passed along to you, the barely-making-rent viewer. Check the eclectic calendar frequently for the next unpolished, undiscovered gem.

THE CATCH

Films are usually $5.

Cinema Heaven Encore

At the Melt Café
700 Columbus Avenue
www.noirfilm.com/Barbara_BelleDiamond.htm

Saturday, 8:00 P.M.

From *Mildred Pierce* to *Double Indemnity,* these classic black-and-white flicks come to life—as much as possible over the roar of a popular Irish-style pub serving pretty good Indian food. Films with a San Francisco theme or location are given prefer-

THE CATCH: Free, but a reservation to belle_diamond@hotmail.com is required, and you may get a hairy eyeball if you don't buy a beer.

ence, but any dusty gem of wisecrackin' dicks and troubled dames will please the loyal crowd of those who love the genre.

TIP: Additional, but somewhat irregular, Thursday-night noir screenings also happen in various locations downtown, but by reservation only. For more information visit www.noirfilm.com/Screenings.htm.

CinemaLit at the Mechanics' Institute

57 Post Street
(415) 393-0100
www.milibrary.org

Friday, 6:30 P.M.

The lovely eighty-seat meeting room of this well-appointed private library makes a social event out of watching a film, encouraging viewers to come to the cafe a half hour before showtime and to stay after the screening for a group discussion. The film is formally introduced from the library's collection of more than 3,000 DVDs and videos that span multiple genres and decades. Expect themes like a salute to John Huston, a tip of the hat to German comedies of the past fifty years,

THE CATCH: Tickets are $7 to the public, free for members. Reservations to rsvp@milibrary.org are required.

or a tackling of sexual politics and identity. Popcorn and refreshments are available, but they are not a distraction from the "salon" feeling of these weekly events.

Conscientious Projector Film Series

Berkeley Fellowship of Unitarian Universalists
1924 Cedar Street, Berkeley
(510) 528-5403

Second or third Friday, 7:00 P.M.

Why is our world so screwed up? And more important, what can we do about it? These are the questions pursued in this regular film series sponsored by the liberal church's Social Justice Committee. Come, get educated, and move on.

THE CATCH — $7 suggested donation (but no one is turned away for lack of funds).

TIP — Subscribe to the film schedule at bfuusjev-subscribe@lists.riseup.net.

The Dark Room Theatre

2263 Mission Street
(415) 401-7987
www.darkroomsf.com

Third Wednesday of the month and every Sunday, 8:00 P.M.

Two cinematic events make visiting this tiny black box worth it for any cheapskate worth his or her weight in ridiculous fun. The third Wednesday of every month is Bad Porn Night, featuring . . . uh, you got it, bam-chicka-wah-wah of the worst variety, seventies style, with the BYOB crowd yelling obscenities, quandaries, or this week's missed therapy session at the screen. "This is not an intellectual salon," the organizers warn. Good thing there's free popcorn. Sunday's Bad Movie Night is an equally vociferous film fest featuring such kitsch mainstays as *Battlefield Earth, Rambo First Blood Part II,* and nearly anything from the Patrick Swayze oeuvre. Promoters promise to take all of the guesswork out of your night and assure guests that "Yes, it will suck."

THE CATCH — Tickets are $5.

Dolores Park Movie Night

20th Street and Dolores
www.doloresparkmovie.org

Second Thursday of each month May to October, dusk

Few things are more wholesome than a cool summer's night under the stars, a Hollywood hit with a local bent, a visit from the Tamale Lady, and your contented pooch at your feet. (Now if you can just figure out how to keep your hound out of the tamales. . . .) For the low, low price of nothing, kick back in lawn chair–and-extra-blanket style and take in favorites like *Funny Girl* or *Mrs. Doubtfire.* Some band usually opens, too, so come early or else sit wa-a-ay in the back, depending on your mood.

Film Night in the Park

Various locations around the Bay Area
www.filmnight.org

Friday and Saturday, 8:00 P.M., May through October

Get on the schedule for this tasteful (and tastefully no-cost) outdoor movie project, courtesy of the San Francisco Neighborhood Theater Foundation and A.P.P.L.E. FamilyWorks. Thirty-two films—and *good* films, too, considering it's all family-friendly cinema—screen in nine parks in seven cities, prime time, with all the burritos and coolers full of beverages that you can carry. The 2006 lineup listed *Walk the Line, Jaws,* and *Best in Show.* Don't forget an extra blanket; this is San Francisco in summer, after all.

Films and Videos at the Public Library

(415) 557-4400
www.sfpl.org/news/events.htm
Times and locations vary

The library is your friend when your wallet is down and out, because, hey, your tax dollars have already paid for the services. When it comes to film and video screenings for adults and kids, the library branches around the city truly offer a great opportunity to cash in. Kids age five and younger are entertained almost daily with a revolving schedule of cartoons and age-appropriate media. And in the evenings adults can glue their eyeballs on everything from classics of Hollywood's golden era, the city's history in cinematic format, or first-run (OK, second-run) releases. The price for all this free media? No popcorn is allowed in the auditorium.

Green Planet Films Monthly Environmental Film Series

At Varnish Fine Arts
77 Natoma Street
(415) 999-0396
www.greenplanetfilms.org

Last Thursday of the month, 8:00 P.M.

The luscious and somewhat stark art gallery space is just folding chairs away from a regular film screening hall. Once monthly this hopping, two-storied gallery gives voice to one of Green Planet's collection of world films with a potent environmental message, such as the story of how a candy company helped to fight the extinction of the bilby, an endangered Australian marsupial, or the plights of the coral-eating crown-of-thorns starfish. Sometimes, even in nature, truth is stranger than fiction.

TIP Get there early and grab a seat on the couches upstairs. Your butt will thank you.

Goethe-Institut San Francisco
530 Bush Street, Second Floor
(415) 263-8760
www.goethe.de/ins/us/saf/ver/flm/enindex.htm

THE CATCH

Tickets are $5, free for students and members of the GISF.

} Modern German culture in cinematic form—sometimes subtitled, sometimes not. Special World Cup screenings also take place here, and on-theme refreshments are served.

Humanist Hall
390 27th Street, Oakland
(510) 393-5685
www.HumanistHall.net

Wednesday, 7:30 P.M.

This progressive church has been dedicated to "communitarian ideals committed to action for social justice" since 1935, and part of spreading the good word about the military-industrial complex, the filth of abuses of power and wealth, and other left-wing ideology comes forth in a weekly film series. Expect to get angry while

THE CATCH

$5 donation sometimes required.

} watching spirited, underground political rants on everything from the travesties of U.S. foreign policy, the evils of NASA, and the power of nonviolent revolution—all meant to inspire the soul to shape a better world.

Istituto Italiano di Cultura
425 Washington Street, Suite 200
(415) 788-7142
www.sfiic.org

The regular Tuesday-night film series is free only with Istituto membership, but the public is entirely welcome to other, more random screenings that take place roughly twice a month. Unsurprisingly, the films are either classic Italian cinema (such as a recent tribute to Mastroianni) or from the more modern era. Expect Italian with English subtitles, English with Italian subtitles, or, on occasion, just the plain ol tongue of the boot.

Julia Morgan Center for the Arts
2640 College Avenue, Berkeley
(510) 845-8542
www.juliamorgan.org

THE CATCH

Each ticket carries a $5 suggested donation.

} Mostly family focused, this active and beautiful theater sometimes offers its stage to the silver screen. Expect classics like *Citizen Kane* or kid-centric cinema like *Mulan* on a periodic schedule.

La Peña Cultural Center

3105 Shattuck Avenue, Berkeley
(510) 849-2568
www.lapena.org

This Latin-themed cultural center focuses on music and poetry events, but it also hosts film events like the small but proud International Latino Film Festival, the Arab Women Film Series, and the International Disability Film Festival, all showcased at sliding-scale rates. View the online calendar to find out what's happening now.

Mob-Mov

Various locations, Berkeley
www.mobmov.org

Short for "mobile movie," this cinematic happening for artistic tightwads is the bastard child of a drive-in movie theater and a flashmob. Visit the Web site and sign on to the mailing list for the Berkeley shows: It's the only way you'll find out what films are playing, when, and where. The day before a screening, you'll be directed toward some sketchy lot in Berkeley for a viewing of *Run Lola Run* or *The Big Lebowski,* plus free candy, soda, and chips (more often than not). Viewers tune in to a radio station for the soundtrack and voilà—instant drive-in. This is guerrilla theater at its best, enjoyed from the comfort of your own auto's bucket seats. Come on, live a little! Even a Cheap Bastard like you could impress a date at an outing like this.

THE CATCH: Tickets are $5 and up.

Monday-Night Film Series

Zeitgeist Bar
199 Valencia Street
(415) 255-7505

Second Monday in June, July, and August; call for times

Weather permitting, this classic biker bar hosts a summertime outdoor film festival of locally made cinema in its mammoth beer garden. It's a perfect midweek evening, and the crowds flow in as freely as the outstanding house-made Bloody Mary's and pitchers of brew poured behind the bar. Drinks are cheap and you will want one. The smell of the barbecue pit is too good to resist, and well-priced grilled meat kicks Sno-Caps' butt any day.

TIP: Get there early to grab your spot at the vast and packed picnic tables.

The Parkway Speakeasy Theater
1834 Park Boulevard, Oakland
www.picturepubpizza.com

This is a great house, featuring comfy seating, a full menu, and beer by the pitcher, which, depending on the movie, might be the real attraction. Take note of the special features, such as a regular family night and *The Rocky Horror Picture Show* on weekends.

THE CATCH } $5 admission at all times, but matinees are just three bucks. This house is cash only, so don't expect to chalk up any airline miles while you're here.

The Red Vic
1727 Haight Street
(415) 668-3994
www.redvicmoviehouse.com

A worker-owned collective, this neighborhood landmark has been around since 1980 (though its original location is just a few blocks away). This is a full-time art house and second-run movie theater with organic snacks, nutritional yeast for the 'corn, and rows of comfy, padded bench-style seating for those who get there early enough to claim them. Cult and underground classics are a mainstay of the Red Vic repertoire, and the audience never tires of *American Astronaut, City of Lost Children,* or documentaries on 1970s punk bands.

THE CATCH } Tickets are $8 for adults, $4 for seniors and children; $6 for adults for 2:00 P.M. matinees.

TIP Buy a punch card for four admissions for $25.00 (equivalent to $6.50 a ticket). Cardholders can use up to two admissions per show.

Roxie Cinema and the Little Roxie
3117 16th Street
(415) 863-1087
www.roxie.com

Proudly proclaiming to be the longest continually running theater in the city, this 1913 relic has seen better days—and it made a big stir when it was purchased by New College after threat of financial failure. Still, the beloved Rox chugs along, and it opened a tiny second screen just two doors down (though popcorn must be purchased at the main theater, and the second screen isn't much larger than your TV). The seats are really comfy at this noteworthy art house for underground and local cinema, and kudos to them for being a great supporter of independent film from far and wide.

THE CATCH } Tickets are $8 for adults, $4 for seniors and children.

TIP Buy a punch card for six admissions for $26.00 ($4.25 per ticket)—cash only, and only at the theater window a half hour before showtime. Cardholders can use only one admission per person.

THE CHEAP BASTARD'S LOTTERY
(WHERE YOU MAY ACTUALLY WIN)

Penny-pinchers aren't about to blow their cash wad on a long-shot lottery ticket, but winning tickets to movies, theater, museums, club nights, dinners out, and so on is a horse worth a bet. Of course there are no guarantees, but with the exchange of a bit of your contact info to the marketing department (and perhaps a tiny shred of your dignity), local media venues that give away freebies every week are bound to fork over something to you eventually. Here are the local venues that give away a whole lot of stuff to a smallish audience, thus increasing the likelihood of free goods for the truly tight and persistent.

KUSF request line, *(415) 751-KUSF. This radio station of the University of San Francisco is college radio at its best and entirely plugged in to the world of no cover charges for live, small-venue rock shows and the occasional movie pass for intrepid callers. Projecting just 3,000 watts, its daytime listeners are likely to get through and win entry to something interesting that night. Listeners can subscribe to the mailing list for upcoming free events: kusf_fyi-subscribe@yahoogroups.com.*

San Francisco Bay Guardian, *www.sfbg.com/promo/emaillist.html. Add your name to the mailing list to find out about free film screenings, music events, and bar happenings with free and low-cost drinks and prize giveaways.*

SFStation.com, *www.sfstation.com/giveaways. Sign in and win dinners at nice places, free guest listings for fancy club nights, movie passes, DVDs, theater tix, museum entrance, festival tickets, and more.*

University of California at Berkeley Art Museum and Pacific Film Archive

2575 Bancroft Way, Berkeley
(510) 642-0808
www.bampfa.berkeley.edu

Ticket sales: daily 11:00 A.M. to 5:00 P.M.

The Hollywood blockbuster need not apply here. Cerebral entertainment runs the gamut from ancient Japanese puppet animation of Kihachiro Kawamoto to a tribute to smoky French actress Isabelle Huppert, and students and the college-minded clamor for the half-priced seats that you won't find at the megaplex. The house also features arty video screenings, such as festivals of women documentarians and amateur film festivals, with the films' artistic visionaries often available for discussions and Q&As in person.

THE CATCH

Tickets are $8 for adults; $4 for members and UCBerkeley students; $5 for UCBerkeley faculty and staff and for all other students, seniors, people with disabilities, and youth under age seventeen. Additional features are $4. Free the first Thursday of the month at 5:30 P.M.

Yerba Buena Center for the Arts Screening Room

701 Mission Street
(415) 978-ARTS (2787)
www.ybca.org

Wednesday through Sunday, 7:30 P.M.

This eclectic cinematic space is a true bargain for museum members, and unlike most cheap seats, these are actually comfortable, sophisticated, and will give your mind a workout instead of your tush and spine. Make yourself smarter in less than two hours with pleasures the likes of the Human Rights Watch International Film Festival and more esoteric arty celluloid, such as a series on "outsider" artist documentaries, a Swedish showdown of films in real time, and psychedelic light shows from the 1960s. Groovy, baby.

THE CATCH

Tickets are $7 to $8; $5 for students, seniors, and teachers; $5 for YBCA members.

TIP

Pick up a YBCA Film Card. Get it punched for six visits and your next film is free.

SF FILM FESTIVALS: THE MOST NOTEWORTHY EVENTS, AND HOW TO VOLUNTEER TO SEE THEM FOR FREE

DocFest, www.sfindie.com. May. Curated by the same group that organizes the San Francisco IndieFest, this has a similar vibe but focuses on documentary cinema. To volunteer, e-mail info@sfindie.com.

MadCat Women's International Film Festival, www.madcatfilm festival.org. September and October. An unpretentious, experimental collection of film, video, and more from around the globe. To volunteer, click on www.madcatfilmfestival.org/festival_info_volunteer.html or e-mail info@mad catfilmfestival.org.

San Francisco Independent Film Festival, www.sfindie.com. February. A loose, low-key, Mission District–centric film gathering celebrating young and bold DIY film and video. To volunteer, e-mail info@sfindie.com.

San Francisco International Asian American Film Festival, (415) 863-0814, ext. 213; www.asianamericanfilmfestival.org. March. The largest annual exhibition of its kind, showing 130 films in San Francisco, Berkeley, and San Jose. To volunteer, visit www.asianamericanfilmfestival.org/attending/volunteer.php.

San Francisco International Film Festival, (415) 561-5019; www.sffs.org. Two weeks every spring, since 1957. This fesitval attracts 80,000 people to more than 200 films. To volunteer, log on to www.sffs.org/about/volunteer .html or e-mail volunteer@sffs.org.

San Francisco International LGBT Film Festival, www.frameline.org. June. Since 1977 this high-quality collection of queer films has delighted audiences of 70,000 or more. E-mail through the Web site to volunteer.

San Francisco Jewish Film Festival, www.sfjff.org. July and August. Amid a host of other year-round projects, this Bay Area–wide event has launched similar festivals across the nation. To volunteer, e-mail jewish film@sfjff.org.

{ READINGS: }
F R E E   V E R S E

"Diligence is the basis of wealth,
and thrift the source of riches."

–Chinese proverb

Porn, science fiction, memoir, poetry—everyone with a computer or a pen can call themselves a writer, and many of them, from authors of *New York Times* best sellers to brand-new cellar dwellers, are very good. Sure, the big names always come to town to peddle their new hardback, but any word wranglers who can string two words together can find themselves in front of a small crowd and a microphone sharing their creative muse. Readings and spoken-word events fill the steamy air of grimy coffee shops, upscale bookshops, the early evenings of popular bars, and any ol community space where aficionados of the written word gather to sip, listen, and participate. No one is looking to get rich from his art, thus this is one of the city's bumper crops of cheap and low-cost entertainment. Don your thinking cap and dive into the pages of one of San Francisco's greatest brainy resources.

K'Vetch Open Mike

Sadie's Flying Elephant
491 Potrero Avenue (at Mariposa)
(415) 551-7988

First Sunday of the month, 8:00 P.M.; sign-up begins at 7:30 P.M.

Musician Tara Jespen and Tribe 8 mouthpiece and writer Lynnee Breedlove cohost this long-term, well-loved, fifteen (or less) minutes of fame opportunity for a hodge-podge of talent, no matter how talented they may be, at this long-standing Potrero bar with the best name ever. Come and soak it all in, as much of it is too good to miss.

Queer Open Mike

Three Dollar Bill Cafe
1800 Market Street (at Octavia)
(415) 503-1532
www.threedollarbill.com/events/openmic.php

Second and fourth Fridays of the month, 8:00 P.M.; sign-up at 7:30 P.M.

Bitch magazine is the recipient of the proceeds from this event that draws quite a crowd to this cafe on the first floor of the San Francisco LGBT Community Center, and copious bitching is what these writers and poets do. Poetry slams through the walls, and literary musings crawl up from the floorboards. This stage welcomes the talents of established wordsmiths, like Lynnee Breedlove and Daphne Gottlieb, and emerging talent as well.

THE CATCH

} $1 to $5 donation requested.

The RADAR Reading Series

San Francisco Public Library Main Branch
Latino/Hispanic Reading Room, Basement Level
100 Larkin Street (at Grove)

One Tuesday a month, 6:00 P.M. sharp

Powerfully prolific host and deeply enmeshed author Michelle Tea gathers a monthly panoply of talented queer and left-wing underground writers "with the occasional superstar" to dazzle the lyric fantastic at this regular happening. Participants might include a Sri Lanken queer activist, interviews of Israeli and Palestinian relations, and well-known well loveds like Beth Lisick and Portland, Oregon's Ariel Gore. The mandatory Q&A that follows each reading is chided along by free cookies for every question, baked by the multitalented Miss Tea herself. To join the mailing list, e-mail SFSunday@aol.com.

Sacred Grounds Cafe

2095 Hayes Street
(415) 387-3859
www.sacredgroundscafe.com

Wednesday evening

Lo and behold, some of SF's most talented poets read during this regular weekly showcase. There is no admission cost, but decent souls will buy a cup of coffee to keep the venue hot.

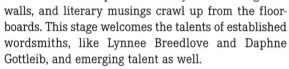

LITQUAKE

www.litquake.org

This star-studded literary event simply cannot be missed, as there's too much happening to ignore. Hundreds of best-selling and semifamous names in every book genre, from mystery to fiction to politics to food and even to children's books, meet with their audience for intimate readings, workshops, panel discussions, and more. Tune in to this year's schedule. Better yet, volunteer to truly hobnob with the Bay Area, and the nation's, literary elite.

Smack Dab
Magnet
4122 18th Street
(415) 581-1600
www.magnetsf.org

Third Wednesday of the month, show at 8:00 P.M.; sign-up at 7:30 P.M.

This is a true open mike night—meaning that anyone is welcome to walk in and read/perform the words, music, comedy, etc., to their heart's content for five whole minutes in the spotlight, though the Castro location and the popular gay writers who host the night tend to give most material a bit of a bend. Author Kirk Read and great event-list congregator Larry-Bob Roberts usher in the unexpected and, they proudly proclaim, "make the Castro safe for performance again." It's not a bar, so all ages are welcome.

The Speakeasy Reading Series
A Night of Poetry at the Bazaar Cafe
5927 California Street (at Twenty-first Avenue)
http://speakeasyreadings.com

First Sunday of the month, 6:00 P.M.

Host Regan Douglas gathers together a handful of poetry-centric Bay Area spoken-word artists to share their work with a mellow, caffeine-sipping, appreciative crowd of the same.

The Word Party

At Club Deluxe
1511 Haight Street
(415) 552-6949
www.thewordparty.com

Tuesday, 8:30 P.M. to midnight

Open mike poetry and jazz just meld into one another at this swing-era venue that suits the mood. This welcoming party is well organized, well attended, and would surely make any soulful beatnik consider cracking a smirk in delight.

THE CATCH

There is a one-drink minimum.

Writers with Drinks

The Make-Out Room
3225 22nd Street (at Valencia)
www.writerswithdrinks.com

Second Saturday of the month, 7:30 to 9:30 P.M.; doors open at 7:00 P.M.

What variety meat is to lunch, WWD is to the literary scene. This stage, graced by SF's sexiest tranny and well-polished writer, Charlie Anders, is a hodgepodge test-tube baby of what happens when erotica meets free verse, collides with stand-up comedy, and rams into the rear of speculative fiction. Arrive early—the comfy tables always fill—and cruise this essential gathering for the literary set. Names on the roster have included Daniel Handler, Andrew Sean Greer, Annie Sprinkle, and many more. All proceeds benefit Anders's pet project, *Other Magazine*.

THE CATCH

$3 to $5, sliding scale

Yerba Buena Gardens Festival

760 Howard Street
(415) 543-1718
www.ybgf.org

May through October

Multiple free literary events are on the calendar for this summerlong free festival. See page 46 for more information.

Youth Speaks

www.youthspeaks.org

Various times and locations

For ten years teens and kids have been encouraged to write and speak their mind and tell their story through vibrant peer groups and leadership. There's always something to be heard at their often-boisterous gatherings, held poetry-slam style, and their credits include a packed calendar of events that take place in coffee shops, street festivals, and printed publications with a hip-hop air. Almost all performances are free.

GREAT BOOKSTORES THAT REGULARLY HOST AUTHOR READINGS AND BOOK SIGNINGS

If they're on tour, you'll find them here. . . .

Black Oak Books, *1491 Shattuck Avenue, Berkeley; (510) 486-0698; www.blackoakbooks.com. Note that they have two locations in SF–in the Sunset and in North Beach–but that all bookstore events happen at this Berkeley location.*

The Book Passage, *1 Ferry Plaza, #46 (Market at Embarcadero); (415) 835-1020; www.bookpassage.com. Note that most events take place at the Corte Madera flagship store in Marin County, but that many readings happen at this store in the Ferry Building.*

Books Inc.; *www.booksinc.net. This left-coast bookstore chain has a number of locations–including two in the airport–but a slew of events occur at these SF spots:*

• Books Inc. in the Castro, 2275 Market Street; (415) 864-6777

• Books Inc. in the Marina, 2251 Chestnut Street; (415) 931-3633

• Books Inc. in Laurel Village, 3515 California Street; (415) 221-3666

Booksmith, *1644 Haight Street; (415) 863-8688; www.booksmith.com.*

City Lights Bookstore, *261 Columbus Avenue (at Broadway); (415) 362-8193; www.citylights.com.*

Modern Times Bookstore, *888 Valencia Street; (415) 282-9246; www.mtbs.com.*

Stacey's Bookstore, *581 Market Street; (415) 421-4687; www.staceys.com.*

{THEATER:}
THE CHEAP SEATS

"This was a way to thrive, and
he was blest; And thrift is blessing,
if men steal it not."

—*William Shakespeare*

Though San Francisco's grand theatrical dames are no Great White Way, superpricey showstoppers can still be a free, or nearly free, ticket for the intrepid Cheap Bastard willing to work a bit for the fruits of the stage. If you like your theater smaller and darker, myriad actors' hothouses are tucked into nooks and crannies that offer great, innovative, or, er, interesting staged theatrics on the cheap. Tune in to the right deals and it's easy to save a buck or two if your schedule is a little flexible.

JUST PLAIN FREE THEATER

Free Shakespeare in the Park
P.O. Box 460937, San Francisco 94146-0937
(415) 558-0888, (800) 978-PLAY
www.sfshakes.org

This theatrical tempest swarms into a midsummer afternoon's dream of culture, gratis. Bring your own blanket, picnic, and Olde English–to-English dictionary to fully appreciate the splendor of this highly acclaimed company's community freebies that are to be (or not to be) in various parks around the region.

San Francisco Free Civic Theater
(415) 337-4713
www.sffct.org

A division of San Francisco Recreation and Parks, this adult theater company produces three to four shows that run from September through May. All participants are volunteer, and performances don't cost a dime. Most shows play at the Randall Museum Theater or the Eureka Valley Recreation Center Auditorium. Get in touch to find out what's playing or to get involved.

San Francisco Mime Troupe

855 Treat Avenue
(415) 285-1717
www.sfmt.org

Since 1959 this political, satirical, and musical institution has been sticking it to the policymakers of contemporary life with full-blown, Tony Award–winning performances, scores, sets, and costumes. Contrary to what the name would indicate, this is not a showcase of whiteface mimes; rather, the subject of their stage is a broken-mirror mimicry of the current state of political affairs. The new season always debuts July Fourth weekend at SF's Dolores Park to a crowd of thousands and then tours into early fall at parks and outdoor venues in the Bay Area and beyond.

THE CATCH: Donations are requested, and a hat is passed at the end of every show.

San Francisco Theater Festival

Yerba Buena Gardens, Yerba Buena Center for the Arts, and Zeum
Between 3rd and Mission Streets and 4th and Howard Streets
(415) 543-1718
www.sftheaterfestival.org

One day a year during summer, this all-day three-ring circus of local theater strives to expose audiences to a taste of the entire theater community, and there just aren't enough hours to see it all. From Shakespeare to Beatles' songs, from improv to puppet shows to one-act plays, ten stages quickly rotate the scaled-down performances of seventy different troupes, companies, and groups of practicing performers and shed the spotlight on the broader, SF theater community.

TIP: This is a great place to pick up discount coupons for theatrical performances throughout the year.

Woman's Will

(510) 420-0813
www.womanswill.org

Summer, usually July through August

Ever heard of Shakespeare's sister? If she had started her own, all-female Shakespeare company, it might look something like this—women run and operated, and defying the ancient tradition of men playing all of the best women's roles. The entire Bay Area is treated to this intensely flavored summer stock; check the schedule for this year's events.

THE CATCH: It's free, but donations are encouraged.

WILL WORK FOR THEATER— USHERING OPPORTUNITIES

American Conservatory Theater (A.C.T.)

415 Geary Street

(415) 439-2349 (volunteer hotline)

One of the city's most prestigious houses—and the only one to offer New York–style free show access in exchange for showing paying patrons to their seats. It's a beautiful and dramatically vertical theater (if you get stuck on the third balcony, you might as well wait and rent the DVD). For the low, low price of nothing, alert theater fans who give the hotline ten to twelve days' notice can request to work showing folks to their seats (and yes, sometimes that means hoofing it up all of those stairs) in exchange for lingering on to see the show gratis.

Cal Performances

Events at Zellerbach Hall, Hearst Greek Theatre, Wheeler Auditorium, and Alfred Hertz Hall

(510) 643-6710

http://cpinfo.berkeley.edu/information/job/volunteer.php

The only thing better than seeing exquisite performances like *MacHomer, Waiting for Godot,* and *Gilberto Gil* and a panoply of dance, music, theater, and family events is to see them without disturbing the dust on your wallet. Those willing to sing for their supper (well, sort of) can try to score one of the coveted ushering gigs in exchange for seeing the show smack-dab in the center of the UCBerkeley campus. Volunteers usually show up ninety minutes before curtain in the requisite white button-down shirt, black bottoms, and black shoes. Just before the show begins, any remaining seats are yours, but you must be back on the clock during intermission.

Eureka Theatre

215 Jackson Street

(415) 255-8207

www.42ndstmoon.org

Home to theater company 42nd Street Moon in the Yerba Buena Center for the Arts, this little company that could specializes in classic musical revivals, equipped with fantastic costumes and memorable and efficient sets. It boasts a mighty Wurlitzer and all the fixin's of picture-show heaven. Volunteer ushering is informal: Call the number above and find out which upcoming dates have openings. Show up an hour before curtain, dressed in the requisite black and white. Help folks find their seat, maybe sell a concession or two, and you're in.

Herbst Theater

401 Van Ness Avenue (at McAllister Street)

http://sfwmpac.org/topnav/general_info.html

As part of the San Francisco War Memorial and Performing Arts Center, this massive, bustling theater hosts a tremendous amount of theatrical and performing arts happenings, including live discussions with notable celebrities, dance, music, and, of course, grand theatrical stagings beneath its classic red-velvet curtain. Volunteers should arrive at the door to the left of the box office ninety minutes before showtime. Black business attire is required (including white dress shirt and black tie for men), as is a flashlight.

THE CATCH No advanced arrangements for ushering are accepted; first come, first served.

Post Street Theatre

450 Post Street

(415) 321-2909

www.poststreettheatre.com

With tickets running as high as $85 a pop, you'll be happier to part with your time than your dollars. Groups of up to four people are often able to work together—and then see the show—at this top-notch, often-overlooked, first-class showplace. Call the number above and leave your contact info and preferred dates.

DISCOUNTS AT SPECIFIC THEATERS

Berkeley Repertory Theater

2025 Addison, Berkeley

(510) 647-2949, (888) 427-8849

www.berkeleyrep.org

The Rep offers a number of ways for students and the general public to save money on theater tickets. First, there's HotTix, a limited number of half-priced show tickets (limit two per customer) that can be purchased directly from the box office, in person, Tuesday through Friday beginning at noon after opening night. Anyone under the age of thirty can purchase half-priced advance tickets, online or in person, for any show excluding prime time—Friday and Saturday night and Sunday matinees. Be prepared to show proof of age. Students and seniors over the age of sixty-five can also buy half-priced tickets a half hour before any show, based on availability, cash only. Other discount programs apply to alumni members and groups of fifteen or more.

THE CATCH Opportunities for half-priced shows have certain restrictions.

Magic Theater

Fort Mason Center, Building D, Third Floor
(415) 441-8822
www.magictheatre.org

Tuesday nights in season

One day a week tickets are sold on a sliding scale, and fans of the cheap seats can see a show for as little as $5 (or as much as $5 million). Group discounts are available for most shows—10 to 15 percent off for six or more tickets purchased together. With just 162 seats, there's not a bad spot to see the stage.

THE CATCH: The theater is sometimes rented out to external productions, including for most of the summer, in which case a discount does not apply.

New Conservatory Theatre

25 Van Ness Avenue
(415) 861-8972
www.nctcsf.org

Every production at New Conservatory has one night that's open to the cash-strapped theater fan. On these special sellout nights, attendees may pay what they can afford directly at the box office at 6:00 P.M. Check the calendar to learn about upcoming cost-saving nights.

THE CATCH: Cash sales only, with a maximum of two tickets per person.

San Francisco State University's College of Creative Arts

McKenna Theatre, Creative Arts Building
1600 Holloway (at Nineteenth Avenue)
(415) 338-2467
www.collegeofcreativearts.org/about/ticketing.html

Click here to print out a coupon good for two tickets for the price of one. This offer applies to all SFSU student performances but only to certain third-party events taking place at the CCA. Call to make sure this offer is valid for the event you'd like to attend.

THE CATCH: Must purchase two-for-one tickets, and not all performances are eligible.

REHEARSAL SPACES
ON THE CHEAP

The Jon Sims Center for the Performing Arts (1519 Mission Street; www.jonsimsctr.org) hosts a few events on-premises, but its primary goal is to house affordable rehearsal space for a wide array of queer artists and performers who can't afford to pay for it. Through a work-exchange program—participants work twelve hours per month in exchange for the same amount of access time to the space for rehearsal—burgeoning artists can tap into a network of like-minded talents and find ways to showcase their talents. Five slots are available every four months. Interested parties should contact Jon Sims for details of the application process.

SMALLER, INEXPENSIVE ART HOUSES

These venues or traveling troupes feature shows that usually cost around $20 or less. Check what they're offering this season.

Custom-Made Theater Company, 965 Mission Street; (415) 896-6477; www.custommade.org.

Exit Theater, 156 Eddy Street; (415) 249-9332; www.theexit.org, www.sffringe.org. They also need lots of see-for-free volunteers for the Fringe Festival in September.

Intersection for the Arts, 446 Valencia Street; (415) 626-2787; www.theintersection.org.

The Marsh, 1062 Valencia Street; (415) 826-5750, (800) 838-3006; www.themarsh.org. Note that they also have an East Bay location: the Marsh Berkeley, in the Gaia Arts Center, 2118 Allston Way, Berkeley. Volunteer ushering opportunities are available for some performances.

San Francisco Playhouse, 536 Sutter Street; (415) 677-9596; www.sfplayhouse.org. Previews are just $18.

Shelton Theater, 533 Sutter Street; (415) 433-1227; www.sheltontheater.com.

Theater Rhinoceros, 2926 16th Street; (415) 861-5079; www.therhino.org.

Victoria Theatre, 2961 16th Street; (415) 863-7576; www.victoriatheatre.org.

MAILING LISTS/DISCOUNTS

Goldstar Events Newsletter
www.goldstarevents.com

Their promise: For the price of a movie, registered users can view live entertainment, almost all of it half price, and some of it entirely free. Don't expect an 8:00 P.M. Saturday show, but if your schedule is willing to bend, you can easily pick the low-hanging theatrical fruit at a pauper's price. Customize the information you receive based on what kind of stage show you'd like to see. Goldstar will also send you special deals for musical events, spa services, and more. A small processing fee applies for each purchase.

Tix Bay Area
Powell Street, between Union and Post (Union Square)
www.theatrebayarea.org/tix/tix_booth.jsp

Same-day half-price tickets go on sale here every day, except for Thanksgiving, Christmas, and New Year's, beginning at 11:00 A.M. The lines can be long in the morning, when ticket selection and seats are at their prime.

Tix Bay Area Online
http://tix.theatrebayarea.org/Wt4/wc.dll?Webtix~NewForm~Events3.wcs

Oddly enough, and just to confuse you, this online Tix booth has a different selection of shows than its physical location in Union Square. Easy to use and easy to search, the online service's half-price tickets for same-day shows are available at your fingertips, Tuesday through Saturday, 11:00 A.M. to 5:00 P.M.

{ MUSIC: }
FREE BIRD!

"Money's a horrid thing to follow,
but a charming thing to meet."

—Henry James

Is there any sound sweeter than freedom ringing? Maybe it's the ringing in your ears that you got for cheap? This town is alive with the sounds of nearly any musical genre your brain can muster, from samba to hard rock, acoustic to electronica. The variety of venues to enjoy them in is equally as varied, covering grassy knoll, grungy club, distinguished performance house, and everything in between. Cool or chaotic, start having a foot-tapping or booty-shaking good time at the city's broad offerings of talent to amuse your ears.

BARS, NIGHTCLUBS, AND CAFES WITH LIVE MUSIC AND NO COVER

Abbey Tavern
4100 Geary Boulevard
(415) 221-7767
www.abbeytavern-sf.com

Thursday through Sunday, 9:30 P.M. to 2:00 A.M.

Club Abbey features a college-heavy, mixed, laid-back crowd doing what few will dare to try in a sports bar: dance! And how could they not? DJs Ken Louis and Schrobi-Girl take turns at the deck spinning top-40 and popular club music to a well-inebriated bunch high on life and the really cheap selection of draft beers. The truly penny-pinching will appreciate that on Thursday night, pitchers of Bud are $5 and pints are just a buck. If your two left feet can't jive, there's always the regular assortment of amusements like pool, darts, pinball, and sports on TV.

Amnesia

853 Valencia
(415) 970-0012
www.amnesiathebar.com

Monday, Tuesday, and Wednesday

You'll pay up to ten bucks to witness premium DJs here on the weekends, but mid-week bargains in entertainment are to be had for the intrepid looking for a good time. Monday night is the highly acclaimed bluegrass night, where attendees ease into the week the mountain way and have easy conversation over the acoustic sounds from the tiny stage. On Tuesday you and your friends are free to make fools of yourselves at Rock Out Karaoke. And Wednesday is the entirely underrated gypsy jazz night, where a revolving band of the incredibly talented strum and pluck out 1920s-style jazz good enough to make Betty Boop flit her lashes and go boop-oop-a-doop!

Bazaar Cafe

5927 California Street
(415) 831-5620
www.bazaarcafe.com

Tuesday through Sunday

Cozy, unplugged, and ready to showcase local acts, this is a favorite haunt for the aspiring original musician trying to grow a fan base and gain some performance experience. Thursday nights are open mike, and potential performers need to call or drop by in person to secure their moment in the spotlight. If the crowd goes wild, you may be lucky enough to be invited back to perform another night. The music series is so popular that the cafe has released its own compilation CD of some of its favorite acts.

Brainwash Cafe and Laundromat

1122 Folsom Street
(415) 861-3663
www.brainwash.com

Friday and Saturday, 8:00 P.M.; Sunday through Wednesday, 7:00 P.M.

All musical genres and socializing needs become swirled and agitated at this long-standing SoMa space featuring a great, priced-right cafe; lots of elbow room; a full Laundromat for your dirty dungarees pleasure; and free, all-ages live entertainment every night of the week (though Thursday night features comedy). The quality and style varies—sometimes the show is that dingy unmatched sock that gets stuck in your sheets, other times it's a cool T-shirt score. It's free.

THE CATCH
If you can't spring for a $2.50 beer to enjoy the show, it costs only a quarter to dry.

The Bubble Lounge

714 Montgomery Street
(415) 434-4204
www.bubblelounge.com

Jazz on Tuesday, 8:00 P.M. to midnight; DJs Wednesday through Saturday

Despite the fact that this West Coast outpost of a champagne salon is quite posh, there is never a cover charge to come soak in the effervescent atmosphere, hip jazz on Tuesday, and live, hip, ambient DJs Wednesday through Saturday. Friday night features DJs on both floors, and it's the only time that dancing, rather than conversation, takes center stage. Otherwise, join the ranks of the other bubbly, beautiful people as they revel in an outstanding sparkling wine menu and überchic decor.

THE CATCH | If you want any other niceties, such as a table, bottle service, or valet parking, be prepared to pay through the nose.

TIP | Great for a date.

Dolores Park Cafe

501 Dolores Street
(415) 621-2936
www.doloresparkcafe.org

Friday, 7:30 to 10:00 P.M.

Mostly acoustic musicians, many with an Indigo Girls-y bend, strum to a packed, all-ages house at this popular, parkside venue with lots of seating, caffeine, and beer. Check the online calendar or, better yet, subscribe to the newsletter to find out who's playing this week.

THE CATCH | A hat is passed at every show, and donations for the artist are appreciated.

Gold Dust Lounge

247 Powell Street
(415) 397-1695

Daily, 8:30 P.M.

Open for more years than anyone would care to calculate, this is one of those bars whose happy hour starts at 7:00 in the morning, if you catch the drift, and this will either frighten you or entice you to investigate further. Should you choose the latter, know that the house band, Johnny Z and the Camaros (a revolving foursome of the same twelve-or-so guys) will be there every night until the wee, drunken hours—playing classic rock from the 1950s to 1970s at more decibels than your ears have had to handle in a good, long while.

Johnny Foley's Irish House
243 O'Farrell Street
(415) 954-0777
www.johnnyfoleys.com

Most nights, 9:00 P.M.

This Irish-themed public house has a full lunch and dinner menu, though one needn't buy food to take in the entertainment. It also features a beer list as long as the Dublin winter is cold, and the staff never hits you up for money just for the privilege of walking in the door. The welcoming space features live bands Monday through Saturday, mostly 1960s classic rock, cover bands strumming everything from Garth Brooks to AC/DC and with a few romantic ballads and bluegrass bits thrown in just for show. The current calendar of who's playing resides on the Web site.

Papa Toby's Revolution Cafe and Art Bar
3248 22nd Street
(415) 642-0474
www.myspace.com/revcafe2006

Most nights, 8:00 or 9:00 P.M.

Like the great revolution, the music may happen, and it may not. But when it does, you will be a part of it, and it will move you. This intimate, rickety, super-laid-back conversation joint features tons of outdoor exposure, good coffee, and great sangria. Treat your ears to everything from jazz and tango to sizzling ukulele, string trios, and an eclectic mix of all that can cram into this tiny space.

Pier 23 on the Embarcadero
(415) 362-5125
www.pier23cafe.com

Tuesday through Saturday, 8:00 to 11:00 P.M.

Classic jazz, salsa, reggae, honky-tonk . . . all genres take turns on this free stage popular with Bay-viewing tourists. A menu of seafood specialties, sandwiches, and pub grub rounds out the white-tablecloth experience. The daring can enjoy free salsa dance lessons on Wednesday night.

THE CATCH
Nursing a pricey drink or two is your ticket in.

The Sacred Grounds Cafe Open Mike
2095 Hayes Street
(415) 387-3859
www.sacredgroundscafe.com

Thursday, 7:30 to 10:00 P.M.; sign-up at 7:00 P.M.

Acoustic street musicians gather at this popular Haight-Asbury cafe for the opportunity to attend a musical forum where some come to play and some come to listen. Performers get ten minutes or two songs to strut their stuff. A typical cafe menu of cheap eats, coffee drinks, and the like assure some small contribution for nearly every budget.

Shanghai 1930
133 Steuart Street
(415) 896-5600
www.shanghai1930.com

Monday through Thursday, 7:00 to 11:00 P.M.; Friday and Saturday, 8:00 P.M. to midnight

Quartets, trios—they've got jazz in every conceivable configuration, all with no cover charge, no drink minimum, and rarely a standing-room-only crowd. This upscale Chinese restaurant features lively digs and a crowd to match.

Swig
571 Geary Street
(415) 931-7292
www.swig-bar.com

The calendar is packed with free and fun things to do and free and fun people to do it with. This modern, superstylish hangout has a lot going for it, including spectacular sipping cocktails and a Scotch menu that would make your grandfather from the Highlands proud to wear the kilt. The entertainment, and the host of cushy vantage points from which to strike a pose and enjoy it, makes Swig a destination worth MUNI'ing for. Sunday night is an open blues jam, and Monday night is for live bands of different stripes. Tuesday through Saturday nights reveal stellar turntables a'spinning and booties shaking for Chris Orr the Vinyl Whore, plus indy, pop, eighties, Brazilian funk, dance hall, breaks, etc., throughout the week.

BARS, NIGHTCLUBS, AND CAFES WITH NO COVER FOR SPECIFIC EVENTS

Blondie's Bar & No Grill
540 Valencia Street
(415) 864-2419
www.blondiesbar.com

DJs Sunday, Monday, Wednesday, and Thursday, 9:00 P.M.

Pints of martinis, people . . . *pints! of! martinis!* If that is not an alcoholic cheap-skate's best bulk buy, then you should just tuck a flask into your sock. Pair that with a posing hipster, high-energy Mission crowd of club kids and DJs spinning eighties music at Blondie's Wetspot (ew . . .), their ample dance floor, and you have a party. Or if you prefer it live, local talent graces the stage with funk, Latin, or jazz three nights weekly. Best of all, if you've got 'em, smoke 'em. This is one of the few joints in the city where smokers can light up at will.

The Cellar
685 Sutter Street
(415) 441-5678
www.cellarsf.com

DJs Monday, Tuesday, Wednesday

Suckers shell out at much as $15 here on a weekend, but those in the know can party in style for nothing—if you time it right. Monday and Tuesday are the best nights to hit it, because not only do you get great house-spun dance hall and reggaeton, or old-school hip-hop, but there are $3 beers all night long and other specials on fancy cocktails.

THE CATCH This is a Union Square bar with a dress code, bottle service, and VIP reservations. Enter any other night of the week at your own risk.

Harry Denton's Starlight Room

450 Powell Street
(415) 395-8595
www.harrydenton.com

Live music and DJs Sunday, Monday, and Tuesday, 8:30 P.M.

Deep house and classic R&B smoothly lilt from the turntables Sunday and Monday at this regular DJ and performance bar and restaurant off of tourist-heavy Union Square. Tuesday night, however, features no cover and a live band—usually sultry soul or some other genre to fit the classy joint's plush red decorum.

TIP   Reservations are highly recommended, though reservations are not as critical at midweek events.

The Hotel Utah Open Mike

500 Fourth Street
(415) 546-6300
www.thehotelutahsaloon.com

Monday music, 8:30 p.m; sign-up at 7:30 P.M.

Rich with a century's worth of colorful history, today this low-rent watering hole and beer hall brings in bike messengers and the grumbling, anticorporate set for loads of beer and better-than-average bar food served slowly at reasonable prices. One night a week the revolving wheel of musical talents spins toward a free night for attentive audiences of real music lovers, and those who perform get to do so based on the luck of the draw of the hat. Unlike most open mikes, not everyone performing here is a newbie, and cheapskates will likely hear some good tunes for a song. The show has become so popular that the Hotel Utah has known to host the event at other bars around the city from time to time. Join the mailing list to find out who's up this week. Piano and PA available.

House of Shields

39 New Montgomery Street
(415) 975-8651
www.houseofshields.com

Live music and DJs Tuesday, some Wednesdays, and Thursday

This is one of the few great bars still catering to cheapskates in Downtown's polluted sea of too much posh. Standing for more than a hundred years, the look is pure luxe, with weathered dark wood throughout, high ceilings, cozy red booths, and a baby grand piano in the corner. Monday is happy hour all day, meaning $2 PBRs, $5 wells, and loads of board games to give you something to do while getting schnockered. Even when the hour is not officially "happy," drinks are still totally reasonable, and they often have free (and great) bar snacks available for Friday happy hour. Tuesday, anything goes, but patrons will be treated to some kind of live, piano-based crooner from 5:30 until around 9:00 P.M. Wednesday night is the eclectic Dirty Little Bitches show, and Thursday features turntables spinning the sounds of the last century.

THE CATCH: Friday and Saturday feature live indy, electronica, and pop for a cheap (usually $4) cover.

Il Pirata

2007 16th Street
(415) 626-2626

DJs Sunday and Wednesday, 10:00-ish

This awesome, out-of-the-way Potrero bar is huge, the right amount of divey, and plush with big booths, cheap beer, and decent parking. They host a revolving wheel of events, including salsa music the last Friday of the month, and bouts of live music of various stripes a couple of times a month. But they are best known for their mellow psychedelic trance DJs on Wednesday, and their late-night reggae on Sunday is guaranteed to make you late for work Monday morning. They also serve food, if you're feeling brave.

Ireland's 32

3920 Geary Boulevard
(415) 386-6173
www.irelands32.com

Live music Thursday through Sunday

Wednesday night is open mike night, and Tuesday night is for aspiring comedians, but otherwise there is a live band every night, and more often than not, it won't cost a penny to sit inside, Irish pint in hand. Genres vary and cover everything from traditional Gaelic to American rock 'n' roll.

Madrone Lounge

500 Divisadero Street
(415) 241-0202
www.madronelounge.com

CB Records Presents: Tuesday, 9:00 P.M.

Thug jazz and funk rock from around the world heat up and spin out of control from the decks of these local music makers and shakers. Two-dollar Red Stripes and $3 Jameson shots add just the right reverb.

Octavia Lounge

1772 Market Street
(415) 863-3516
www.octavialounge.com

Sunday through Friday

This large Market Street enclave always has something going on, and rarely will one have to wait for a table to enjoy it. From myriad open mike nights for instrumental artists to jazz quintets and trios to male and female vocalists, the sounds are smooth and nonobtrusive. Most Sunday to Friday evenings, and Sunday afternoons, are free for your listening pleasure. In addition to a celebrity-crooner cocktail menu (try the Nina Simone, made from Kurant & Citrus vodka, Cointreau, lemon juice, and cranberry), the Octavia has a dinner and brunch menu.

THE CATCH } It would be tough to come and hear the show without at least ordering a drink. Expect to shell out a $5 to $10 cover for a Saturday night.

Plough & Stars

116 Clement Street
(415) 751-1122
http://pweb.jps.net/~jgilder/plough.html

Sunday through Thursday, 9:00 P.M.

THE CATCH } Cover charge on weekends.

For traditional Irish music, this is the place, though patrons are just as likely to think about clogging to bluegrass, gypsy jazz, and country acts. Check the calendar to see what's playing.

Rasselas Jazz Club

1534 Fillmore Street
(415) 346-8696
www.rasselasjazzclub.com

Live music Monday through Thursday, 8:00 P.M. to midnight; Sunday, 6:00 P.M. to midnight

A 300-person concert hall; a second, intimate lounge; a fully-stocked Ethiopian restaurant and bar; and all flavors of jazz and related world beat sounds situated at the easily accessible intersection of Fillmore and Geary in the historic Fillmore Jazz district . . . what's not to love about this long-standing, family-run establishment? For the price of a drink or two to enjoy the show, audiences get a cozy, music-centric crowd jamming to Afro-Cuban jazz, melodic vocals, soul and funk, live dub, and more.

THE CATCH | $7 cover on shows for Friday and Saturday nights; otherwise the only cost is the price of a drink or two.

Savanna Jazz

2937 Mission Street
(415) 285-3369
www.savannajazz.com

This mission-driven, community education-minded jazz venue stages live music six nights a week, with only one to two of those nights requiring a cash barrier to entry. The musically minded can also attend periodic lectures and learning series on the genre, provided gratis for those who just want to come and learn. More often than not, lounge lizards are jamming to the quality sounds of the house jazz trio, with a revolving guest repertoire, and the weekly, freestylin', jazz jam session. True aficionados come here for quality, real deal jazz; French, Caribbean, and West African eats; and a rightfully dark, black-turtlenecked ambience.

THE CATCH | Some nights' acts require a cover.

The Skylark

3089 16th Street
(415) 621-9294
www.skylarkbar.com

In the armpit of the Mission, this tiny, dim watering hole has a cozy charm and appeal and live DJs kickin' it seven nights a week (though good luck finding room to shake even a single body part). Seventies and eighties rock, world hip-hop, and old-school funk rule the speakers. Get your buzz on with happy hour every night with drinks just two bucks a pop.

Thee Parkside
1600 17th Street
(415) 503-0393
www.theeparkside.com

It's a Free Country Sunday: 4:00 P.M.

Country, western, bluegrass, rockabilly . . . "If it's got twang, it's our thang." This premier dive bar just gets better at weekend's end when the beer keeps flowing and the sounds can be enjoyed from the airy back patio. Unlike most free musical venues, this house of great sound is known for booking quality entertainment. As always, the Ping-Pong table is free.

ALTERNATIVE VENUES FOR FREE MUSIC

Center for Contemporary Music (CCM) at Mills College
5000 MacArthur Boulevard, Oakland
(510) 430-2191
www.mills.edu

During the academic year, September through April, this school of experimental performers, composers, performers, and unique collaborators holds several free community events that are always something to behold. From African ethnography to sound and fire to a soprano with a piano, there's always a great reason to cross the bay and boost your cultural IQ. Consult the online calendar to see what they're doing this season.

Community Music Center
544 Capp Street
(415) 647-6015
www.sfcmc.org

From classical to jazz to all genres of music worthy of study and refinement, this mission-driven hub of historical musical learning and preservation offers several evenings of mixed-bag entertainment a month, gratis. Audiences can choose from special engagement, faculty ensembles, and student recitals. Check the calendar to see what's on this month.

Grace Cathedral
1100 California Street
(415) 749-6300
www.gracecathedral.org

No matter what your stance on God, Jesus, or religion, everyone loves beautiful buildings and fantastic acoustics. With your ears ready to receive this spirit, your soul will soar during this grand cathedral's periodic performances that are free and open to the public. Events could include anything from gospel choral ensembles to organ concerts on the church's magnificent instrument to an assembly of children's choruses. Check the calendar to see what holy sounds you can treat yourself to this month.

RobotSpeak Sessions
At RobotSpeak
589 1/2 Haight Street
(415) 554-1977
www.robotspeak.com

Every other month

Computer and electronic music come to robotic life at this regular boys-in-baggy-pants event in the Lower Haight's basement record shop. All are welcome to listen and observe as DJs spin their own flavor of turntableism and electronica every other month. Each thirty- to forty-minute set features three performers and allows time for Q&A and technique sharing for other enthusiasts of the electronic San Francisco sound. BYOB and it's a party.

San Francisco Cable Car Chorus
At Grace Evangelical Lutheran Church
Thirty-third Avenue and Ulloa Street
www.sfcablecarchorus.org

Wednesday, 7:15 to 10:15 P.M.

The basement assembly hall is home to the public rehearsals of this acclaimed, long-standing men's barbershop chorus. All are welcome to sit and listen.

San Francisco Chamber Orchestra

www.sfchamberorchestra.org

With performances all over the Bay Area, from Palo Alto to Berkeley to SF, and the vast majority of them free, this band of merry professional musicians is clearly motivated to spread the gospel of classical music to a culture-hungry crowd. If you're not sure if classical music is your cup of chablis, this is a great way to find out. The regular family programs are a great way to introduce young ears to something beyond the scope of Raffi. Concerts are first rate and designed to educate but, by high-art standards, mellow enough not to intimidate. This is one of the area's most uncelebrated gems.

San Francisco Folk Music Club Friday Night Jams

885 Clayton Street
(415) 661-2217
www.sffmc.org

Every other Friday, 8:oo p.m.

The 1,000-members-strong organization devoted to acoustic and folk music from all over the world gathers at this regular event, but all are welcome, either to participate or just to listen. A singing room and two instrumental jam rooms run rampant and freestyle, from when everyone gets there until the last person leaves. Some snacks are provided.

THE CATCH
Donations for snacks are welcomed.

Sea Shanty Sing-alongs on *The Balclutha*

Hyde Street Pier
www.nps.gov/safr/planyourvisit/events.htm

This 301-foot historic National Park Service bathing beauty is the performance space where you are often the star. Spend an unforgettable evening aboard this classic ship singing sea shanties as Captain Ahab intended—except that this is a fully sober songfest, where only coffee, tea, and hot chocolate are served in a mug that you bring yourself. This is an irregular event, but check the online schedule often, as it's worth the wait.

FREE OUTDOOR CONCERTS

Bluegrass Festival

Speedway Meadow
Fulton Street and Twenty-sixth Avenue
www.strictlybluegrass.com

First weekend in October

The one disappointing thing about this mammoth, music-filled festival is that it lasts only a single weekend, because with dozens of performers spread over multiple stages, there's enough entertainment to last a week. This popular outing attracts vendors of food, arts, and crafts; a crowd of thousands; and truly well-known performers who dabble in bluegrass and beyond, such as Dolly Parton, Joan Baez, Billy Bragg, and Linda Rondstadt.

Del Monte Square Courtyard

2801 Leavenworth Street (at Columbus Street)
(415) 771-3112
www.delmontesquare.com

Daily, 11:00 A.M. to 8:30 P.M.

From the heart of Touristville, in the axis of Fisherman's Wharf, comes a stage packed with multiple performances each day, featuring mainly music but also all varieties of performance art and comedy suitable for a family audience. This space has hosted the likes of Robin Williams, Shields and Yarnell, and Jefferson Airplane—though performances of this caliber are few and far between. If you're in the area, it's a great excuse to rest your feet and take in some tunes and a bay view.

The Golden Gate Park Band

Musical Concourse
Roughly Tenth Avenue and JFK Drive, adjacent to the de Young Museum
(510) 530-0814
www.goldengateparkband.org

Sunday, 1:00 P.M., April through October

In what is not only a local but also a national tradition—this concert series has been playing nonstop since 1882—this is two hours of wholesome entertainment at its best. Bring a picnic (but not the pooch!) and plan to spend the day amid stunning gardens of plants from around the globe, with musical accompaniment to match. The well-oiled band covers everything from ethnic explorations to Broadway, swing, opera, marches, classical, and more. Note that the usual performance venue, the Spreckles Temple of Music at the Music Concourse (also in the park), is temporarily closed for construction.

Jewels in the Square

Union Square
Geary Boulevard and Powell Street
(415) 477-2600
www.unionsquarepark.us

This new series began after the renovation of Union Square in 2005. Usually held in summer, it presents a stageful of live musical and miscellaneous entertainment ranging from barbershop quartets to country and from punk rock to religious worship services. A plethora of weekend entertainment abounds, but plenty of happenings are scheduled for the midweek lunchtime crowd.

NextArts Concerts with a Cause

(415) 970-9005
www.nextarts.org

This small but growing nonprofit A/V equipment employment and job-training program has just begun to host outdoor summer concerts—including SF's first-ever nighttime concerts in public parks. Check the schedule for locations and dates.

THE CATCH Shows won't cost you a dime, but they often request a donation of goods for the homeless (such as new socks, underwear, or school supplies) in exchange for jazz, big band, and other performance band favorites.

People in Plazas

(415) 362-2500
www.marketstreet.citysearch.com

Monday through Friday, noon, July and August

These noontime events, sponsored by the Market Street Association, have existed for thirty-plus years and feature more than one hundred concerts to brighten up the workday lunch hour at plazas and parks all over Downtown, SoMa, and the Financial District. Genres can be anything from Latin jazz to blues, swing, or mariachi. Consult the Web site for the full schedule of performances.

San Francisco Free Folk Festival

Roosevelt Middle School
460 Arguello Street
(415) 321-0835
www.sffolkfest.org

During one summer weekend, just as they have for the past three decades, hundreds of volunteer organizers and performers come together to treat a flock of 2,000 to 3,000 enthusiastic appreciators to song, dance, percussion, and traditional folk sounds from world cultures and America's own backyard. Truly, there is something on the mile-long calendar to entertain every taste, including performances and workshops geared toward families, songwriters, choruses, and others. Check the Web site for dates and times.

San Francisco Jazz Festival
(415) 398-5655
www.sfjazz.org
June through October

Thursday evening in Union Square and Wednesday lunchtime at Levi's Plaza are two of the more popular outdoor venues for these nonprofit jazz masters, but the greater Bay Area is a stage during the season of outdoor sound. The caliber of the performers is excellent, and these short and often surprising performances are sublime.

The Stern Grove Music Festival
Nineteenth Avenue and Sloat Boulevard
(415) 252-6252
www.sterngrove.org
Sunday, 2:00 P.M., June through August

Since 1938 the mammoth, underused outdoor expanse of Stern Grove has been home to great music on summer weekend afternoons. Arrive very early, as this is one of the most popular outdoor concert series, attracting the enchanted from around the Bay. From rock and pop performers to the San Francisco Symphony, San Francisco Opera, San Francisco Ballet, and well-known Brazilian performers, there truly is a show for all tastes. It's a wonderful way to spend a Sunday afternoon.

Yerba Buena Gardens Festival
760 Howard Street
(415) 543-1718
www.ybgf.org
May through October

This monster free-fest features hundreds of lively, talented, and (natch) free performances in the lush downtown gardens of this popular cultural center during the broad months of SF summer. Music, concerts, and events take place often, with an emphasis on a lunchtime music series of international sound. Dance, spoken word, literary events, youth and family events, and cultural happenings with a visual arts slant round out the extensive calendar. You'll certainly find something to suit your taste. Check the calendar to find out what's playing.

RECORD STORES THAT REGULARLY HOLD FREE IN-STORE PERFORMANCES

Get on the following mailing lists to learn of free, on-site shows for underground and emerging artists.

Amoeba Records, *1855 Haight Street; (415) 831-1200. 2455 Telegraph Avenue, Berkeley; (510) 549-1125; www.amoebamusic.com*

Aquarius Records, *1055 Valencia Street; (415) 647-2272; www.aquarius records.org*

Rasputin Music, *2401 Telegraph Avenue, Berkeley; (800) 350-8700; www.rasputinmusic.com*

RobotSpeak, *589½ Haight Street; (415) 554-1977; www.robotspeak.com*

LOW-COST AND FREE TICKETS TO LARGE ARENA SHOWS

Cal Performances

For events at Zellerbach Hall, Hearst Greek Theatre, Wheeler Auditorium, and Alfred Hertz Hall

See pages 25–26 for more information on free shows in exchange for ushering.

Craigslist Tickets

http://sfbay.craigslist.org/tix

It's always the luck of the moment on this national buy/sell community bulletin board, but those fortunate few may actually be able to find tix to Madonna or the Padres game for a buck—though most tickets will cost a whole lot more.

FREE-TO-SING KARAOKE BARS

Sip your drink slowly and you have a cheap night out watching friends make that Neil Diamond song happen. Tip your KJ a buck and you'll be sure to sing like a bird.

Amnesia, *853 Valencia Street; (415) 970-0012; www.amnesiathebar.com. Tuesday.*

Annie's Cocktail Lounge, *15 Boardman Place; (415) 703-0865; Tuesday and Saturday.*

The Mint Karaoke Lounge, *1942 Market Street; (415) 626-4726; www.themint.net. Every night.*

Silver Cloud Restaurant, *1994 Lombard Street; (415) 922-1977. Tuesday through Sunday. Despite the name, you don't have to eat here.*

Tango Tango, *1550 California Street; (415) 775-0442. Every night.*

Goldstar Events Newsletter
www.goldstarevents.com

Lots of concert tickets, many of which are half price. See page 29 for more information.

Louise M. Davies Symphony Hall
201 Van Ness Avenue
(415) 503-5325
http://sfwmpac.org/topnav/general_info.html

First-time ushering candidates should call the telephone number above and leave their name and address; a packet containing information about ushering and dress code will be mailed to you. After that, every Monday, this same voice-mail line is updated with dates when ushers are needed. Prospects will be instructed to either show up or sign up.

THE CATCH

} Free admission in exchange for ushering.

Nob Hill Masonic Center

1111 California Street
(415) 292-9150
www.masonicauditorium.com

Some ushering opportunities available, depending on the show. Call the in-house head usher at least a week before performances and inquire if volunteers are needed. Note that fall is an especially busy time ripe with opportunity.

THE CATCH

Free admission in exchange for ushering.

War Memorial Opera House

301 Van Ness Avenue
http://sfwmpac.org/topnav/general_info.html

Those interested in being an usher here must write a letter including name, address, phone number, and a brief account of their interest in ushering and snail mail it to House Manager, War Memorial Opera House, 301 Van Ness Avenue, San Francisco 94102. No telephone or e-mail inquiries are accepted. Prospective ushers will be contacted if desired.

THE CATCH

Free admission in exchange for ushering.

{COMEDY: }
CHEAP SHOTS

"Money is that dear thing which, if
you're not careful, you can squander
your whole life thinking of...."

—*Mary Jo Salter*

Some say that the heyday of San Francisco's comedy scene has passed us by, and that the likes of Robin Williams, Phyllis Diller, and the original Purple Onion were the end of the line decades ago. But judging by the number of comedy events to crop up in recent years, and the reopening of some legendary venues, one thing can be said for certain: San Francisco is ready to yuck it up once again. We, the cash stingy, are not in the business of culture scouting or fortune-telling, and all we want is something to keep our wee brains entertained between beers. But we cannot help but wonder if we're in the midst of the next big wave, or if the joke's on us and we're just all wet. Either way, there's enough to explore right now to tickle our funny bone. Remember—free comedy is nothing to laugh at.

THE FREE FUNNIES

Brainwash Cafe and Laundromat

1122 Folsom Street

(415) 861-3663

Thursday, 8:00 P.M.

Local comedian Tony Sparks hosts this regular, longtime comedy night on a stage well worn with open mike. Full laundry facilities are on premises, and a well-priced cafe make it an affordable, and accessible, access point to the Land of Ha.

The Canvas Gallery

1200 Nineth Avenue

(415) 504-0060

www.thecanvasgallery.com

Tuesday, 7:00 P.M.

Jerry Goldstone is your host on this romp through comedy open mike. Classier and artier than your average coffeehouse, the Canvas Gallery lures many here to try to land their big break.

Comedy Day

Sharon Meadows, Golden Gate Park

www.comedyday.com

Thirty comedians fill one stage for five hours of uninterrupted quality humor while you laze with your butt on the grass. Nifty idea, right? This could be why this event has been tremendously popular, drawing an audience of thousands for twenty-five years. Event organizers offer tourist hotel packages for those coming into town especially for the show. Check the online calendar for details about this year's event.

Foot! Comedian-Led Walking Tours

Meets at Lotta's Fountain, 1 Kearny at Market

(415) 793-5378

www.FOOTtours.com

Since the end of the last century, funny people have been showing the humor-appreciating public around town in their own special way—including the Shake 'n Bake historical walk through the site of the 1906 earthquake, and Hobnobbing with Gobs of Snobs, a romp through Nob Hill. Usually these two-hour traveling comedy routines cost $30, but those with an eye on their online calendar can catch periodic "sample" tours for nothing.

THE CATCH } Reservations are required for the sample tours.

Harvey's

500 Castro Street

(415) 431-4278

Every third Tuesday

The slant is gay humor, the cocktails are fruity and strong, and brave guys stand up among a boisterous, sometime inattentive crowd to strut their funny stuff, with results all over the map.

Improv Slam Music Jam

Off Market Theater

965 Mission Street

(415) 823-4779

www.improvslam.com

Thursday, 8:00 P.M.

No sound is sweeter than that of comedy improv put to music. And here, working comedians and brave volunteers take topic suggestions from the audience and create hilarious (hopefully) musical numbers on the spot. It must be seen to be believed. Cash prizes are awarded for the crowd favorite. Anyone is welcome to sign up to participate.

THE CATCH } Be sure to contact organizers via e-mail before the show or else there's a $5 night-of-sign-up fee.

Kung Pao Kosher Comedy

New Asia Restaurant

772 Pacific Avenue

(415) 522-3737

www.koshercomedy.com

If you're ever stuck in town for the holidays, nothing says Merry Christmas like a mammoth, all-star comedy showcase; a multicourse, lavish Chinese dinner; and a room full of Jews. Hence is the Holy Trinity for this sellout annual event that always delivers delicious eats and well-seasoned, seriously funny professionals. The only thing better would be taking it all in without spending a dime, right? Well, if you have signed up for volunteer ushering, you arrive before the show, they feed you a great meal, and you get a free T-shirt. You show folks to their chairs for an hour or so and then you duck upstairs (in my opinion, the best seats in the house) to enjoy the performance. Make this your own holiday tradition, and it will be a good night for all, and for all a good night.

THE CATCH } Free meal and admission in exchange for ushering.

The Red Victorian Hotel's Peace Cafe

1665 Haight Street

(415) 864-1978

www.redvic.com

Sunday, 7:00 to 8:30 P.M.

The historic bed-and-breakfast of the Summer of Love opens its freak-flag-waving doors to local emerging talent for this regular weekend show. It's offered gratis, though certainly the purchase of a coffee or two would be appreciated.

Sea Biscuit Cafe

3815 Noriega Street

(415) 661-3784

Monday, 8:00 P.M.

The Sunset needs a place to get funny, too, and this neighborhood cafe plays host to a wide array of practicing joke-telling folk tenacious enough to risk stand-up in front of a live, coffeehouse crowd.

CHEAP TICKETS TO MAKE YOU CHUCKLE

All-Pro Comedy Showcase

Cobb's Comedy Club

915 Columbus Avenue

(415) 928-4320

www.cobbscomedyclub.com

Wednesday, 8:00 P.M.

While usually home to such high-gloss national talent as Dave Atell, Jamie Kennedy, and Greg Proops, Hump Day is the night that even the working class can afford a seat. On this special evening every week, fifteen comics, both local and from everywhere else, share the stage and cram in over three hours of entertainment. Ounce for ounce, that's a whole lot of comedy value.

THE CATCH }
$10 door fee, plus a two-drink minimum. Wednesday seats may be discounted, but the two-drink minimum is still in effect.

BATS Improv Theatre

Fort Mason Center, Building B, Suite 350
16 Marina Boulevard
(415) 474-6776
www.improv.org

If you've got the lust for improv, and you don't mind buying your tickets ahead of time online, you can see this well-known theater outfit for as little as five bones (or max out at the door-price high of $20). For twenty-plus years BATS has been making things up onstage at audience suggestion . . . and crowds just can't get enough. The cheap seats usually require a Thursday or Sunday performance, but if you can spread your weekend a little longer, close your eyes and make a wish, it will feel like a Saturday for sure.

THE CATCH

Many shows as low as $5 if you purchase tickets online.

The Dark Room

2263 Mission Street
(415) 401-7987
www.darkroomsf.com

This dark, dank, artist-run theater/performance space/bar/comedy club/movie theater/whatever has one common thread in nearly all of its endeavors: They are pure camp, pure fun, and always something to laugh at. From sketch comedy to cabarets to small-time, locally produced exercises in public bravery that border on the blurry line of good taste and offbeat humor, this is the place to enjoy the show. Check the online schedule for events.

THE CATCH

Most happenings $10 or less.

50 Mason Lounge
50 Mason Street
(415) 398-4129
www.50masonlounge.com

Wednesday through Saturday, 8:00 P.M.

This real live comedy club in bustling Union Square delivers what most of its competitors cannot—a whole lineup of talented, local, knee-slapping talent during prime weekend hours for the price of a movie. It sounds like a good deal, and it truly is a whole lot of bang for your comedy buck. For those who want to make every dollar count, Wednesday-night tickets are just $7.

THE CATCH } Tickets are $10 or less.

Green Room Comedy Club's Green Room Showcase
2801 Leavenworth Street
(415) 674-7567
www.greenroomcomedy.com

Monday through Thursday, 8:30 P.M.

This intimate comedy venue in a touristy neighborhood invites professional comedians to "work out" their new material midweek. Audiences get professional entertainers in a real comedy setting at prices less than half of what they'd pay prime time. Such a deal . . .

THE CATCH } Tickets are $10.

Punch Line Comedy Club
444 Battery Street
(415) 397-7573
www.punchlinecomedyclub.com

Sunday and Monday, 7:00 P.M.

If the early bird catches the worm, then the worm that is latest on the weekends must catch the juiciest specimens. Or something. OK, that metaphor sucked, but these comic specimens are anything but for the birds. Sunday's SF Comedy Showcase tickets are just $7.50, and the Monday Comedy Sessions are a mere $6.00. Both events feature local talent good enough to play this national club. If you can't afford this, stay home and watch *Live from the Apollo*.

THE CATCH } Tickets are $7.50 and under. All shows are for age eighteen and over, and a two-drink minimum always applies.

San Francisco Comedy College Clubhouse

414 Mason Street, #705

(415) 921-2051, (877) 735-2844

www.sfcomedycollege.com

Friday and Saturday, 8:00 P.M. and 10:00 P.M.

Students studying the finer points of comic timing, writing, and the art of stand-up need a guinea pig audience. During these prime-time weekend slots, that audience is you. Like any group of training professionals, results may vary. But it's a cheap ticket in an intimate setting with no drink minimum; in fact, it's BYOB.

THE CATCH: Tickets are $7.

San Francisco Sketchfest

www.sfsketchfest.com

This fantastic annual event is definitely worth checking out, as it brings together a vortex of yuck-makers that are certainly worth a splurge at full price (though most tickets, even at full sail, are still just around twenty bucks). However, our Cheap Bastard tip for you is as follows: Go to the Web site and join the mailing list. Midweek events with slightly sluggish sales are often sold two for one within a few hours or a few days before showtime. You can thank us later.

THE CATCH: Join the mailing list for half-price tickets.

{ DANCE: }
FREE MOVES

"Money is human happiness in the
abstract: he, then, who is no longer
capable of enjoying human happiness
in the concrete devotes his heart
entirely to money."

—Arthur Schopenhauer

Some of us simply cannot wait to get into the studio and cut some rug, while those of us with two left hooves prefer to keep our relationship with dance one of appreciation, not participation. Either way, the expression and beauty of body movement and performance is a rich resource in this town, but with so many organized dance classes and events, one needn't be rich to enjoy it. Shake it, twist it, bend it, arabesque it . . . call it what you like. But from every ethnicity and culture, from formal to street, move to the groove of the dance scene in San Francisco.

DANCE PERFORMANCES

Jon Sims Center for the Arts
1519 Mission Street
(415) 554-0402
www.jonsimsctr.org

The JSDance program caters to aspiring queer dancers and choreographers, giving them the resources to put together their own show, including rehearsal space and a performance venue. In the quest to open up the arts to as wide an audience as possible, the center's pricing structure for most events, including the dance series,

THE CATCH
These are low-cost and sliding scale events, though no one is turned away for lack of funds.

is kept accessible, with some show tickets as low as $5, and the promise that all audience members are welcome, despite their access (or lack of) to cash.

San Francisco Aloha Festival

Lincoln Boulevard (at Anza Avenue)
www.pica-org.org/AlohaFest/index.html

One weekend a year for the past twelve years, thousands of Bay Area residents have been mesmerized by hips swaying like palm trees at this celebration of Polynesian culture focusing on traditional dance and music. A boatload of island crafts, arts, and foods are also available from hundreds of vendors. Sponsored by the Pacific Islanders' Cultural Association, this is a pet-free, family-friendly (meaning no alcohol) event.

San Francisco Ballet

War Memorial Opera House
301 Van Ness Avenue
(415) 865-2000
www.sfballet.org

If everything is beautiful at the ballet, then just imagine the stunning beauty and grace of supercheap, same-day tickets for the most prestigious dance performances in town. Seniors over the age of sixty-eight, students with valid ID, and members of the military can call the box office for discounted same-day show tickets, based on availability. Note that the discount is *not* available for the annual holiday *Nutcracker* extravaganza. Check the schedule for event dates and times.

THE CATCH

Even with a discount, tickets are still $10 to $20.

}

THE PULSE ON DANCE

No one is ever turned away for lack of funds at any event at CounterPULSE (1310 Mission Street; 415-626-2060; www.counterpulse.org), and this includes a wide palette of performances, such as dance, music, film, kids' happenings, mixed media, lectures, kooky art, local history, etc. CounterPULSE is mission driven to incubate grassroots projects and social expression of all stripes, and as long as they can afford to do so, they will bend over backward to serve this public need. They also offer gallery space, artist-in-residence opportunities, affordable space rental and office facilities, and more. No matter what a tightwad you are, spare what you can to ensure organizations like this one continue.

Smuin Ballet

300 Brannan Street
(415) 495-2234
www.smuinballet.org

As one of SF's "other" ballet performance companies, tiny Smuin gets the edge by caring for the community and by making their flavor of ballet affordable to all. They offer all of the usual discounts—for seniors, students, groups of ten or more—and hearty discounts to first-time season subscribers. But in addition, their season holds the promise of several pay-what-you-can nights, and they donate blocks of tickets to community groups who would otherwise not be able to offer their constituents access to the finer arts. This ballet doesn't just have legs. It also has heart.

THE CATCH
Some discounts available.

Yerba Buena Gardens Festival

760 Howard Street
(415) 543-1718
www.ybgf.org

May through October

This summerlong massive festival of world culture features periodic dance performances. See page 46 for more information.

DANCE CLASSES AND PRACTICE SESSIONS

ABADÁ-Capoeira San Francisco Brazilian Arts Center

3221 22nd Street
(415) 206-0650
www.abada.org

Most classes in this butt-kicking Brazilian street art are about twelve bucks a pop, but new students on their first day can purchase a four-class card for just $32—a great way to see if your body is up to the moves. Students age nineteen and younger may be eligible for reduced rates and subsidized classes through a community grant.

THE CATCH
Discounts are for new students. No credit cards are accepted; cash and personal check only.

Alonzo King's LINES Ballet (San Francisco Dance Center)
26 7th Street
(415) 863-3040
www.linesballet.org/dance/index.html

Drop-in classes are usually around $13, but if you're a serious prima ballerina, the $45 membership fee can stuff a lot of cash and goods in your tutu, including a free acupuncture consultation, discounts on massages and chiropractic services, discounts on dance-related tickets and merchandise, and, best of all, multiclass passes for as little as $9 each. Also note: The Dance Center opens its heart and its space to the greater dance community by allowing free use of the conference room (with a large table, ten chairs, and monitor with VHS and DVD) by reservation; call extension 221.

THE CATCH } Discounts and free stuff are available with a $45 membership.

Ballroom Dancing
Covenant Presbyterian Church
321 Taraval Street
(415) 664-5335

Monday and Tuesday, 7:30 P.M.

Your instructors, Bill and Dee Dee, are pure poetry in motion as they demonstrate the likes of the American-style cha-cha, waltz, tango, or, on occasion, the hustle. Learners of all ages can only hope to emulate their grace. Beginners are welcome to drop by anytime.

THE CATCH } Admission is $6.

Barefoot Boogie

City Dance Studios
32 Otis Street
(415) 820-1452
sfbarefootboogie.com

Sunday, 7:30 P.M.; Wednesday, 8:30 P.M.

There are a lot of "no's" associated with this event—no cameras, no food, no drinks (other than water), no scents, no smoking, no judgments, and, of course, no shoes. By casting all of these shackles to movement to the side, organizers hope to create a comfy, funky, eclectic space filled with world music from real DJs, true motion and body expression, and a rare opportunity for one to truly shake one's thing.

THE CATCH The first-timer discounted fee is $5.

Fat Chance Belly Dance

670 South Van Ness Avenue
(415) 431-4322
www.fcbd.com

Tuesday, Friday, and Saturday

Nothing is sexier than those swaying hips of fury—particularly when those hips have a little meat on their bones. The teachers of this critically acclaimed, internationally performing troupe offer drop-in classes three days a week for every level of interest and ability, and it's a fat chance that you won't have a good time trying to look as good as they do. Proper attire is required, such as loose, low pants, skirts, or hip scarves. Zils (finger cymbals) are required—bring your own or buy them there.

THE CATCH Admission is $10.

Harvey Milk Recreational Arts Building

50 Scott Street
(415) 554-9523
http://parks.sfgov.org

Hands down, this is the best dance bargain in the city, as a dozen or so classes are taught six days a week in all varieties—tap, country line dancing, capoeira, folk, and creative movement for children and adults—for nothing or next to nothing. The schedule changes seasonally, so check the Web site or pick up a copy of the activities guide to find courses to suit your interest. Almost all are drop in. While a few classes are housed in other rec centers throughout the city, this is the main hub of the dance department. Truly these courses bring the arts into the reach of those at every level of income.

THE CATCH Most classes free; some cost up to $4.

Lindy in the Park

Golden Gate Park
JFK Drive between Eighth and Tenth Avenues
www.lindyinthepark.com

Sunday, 11:00 A.M. (lesson at 12:30 P.M.)

Prolific and skilled lindy dance teacher Hep Jen and her sidekick DJ Ken Watanabe take their dance lessons out of the club and into the open air for this completely fun, free, and informal weekly affair among the trees. The music plays until 3:00 P.M., with a short lesson in between to give park dwellers a few moves to swing by. The best part is that there's nothing to buy, there's no obligation to do anything further, and visitors are welcome week after week. Note that cars are not allowed in the park on Sunday.

Hep Jen and Ken Watanabe have added a second dance freebie, Lindy in the Square. It's the same deal as Lindy in the Park, except it's held in Union Park from 6:00 to 8:00 P.M. on the first Wednesday of every month, May through October.

The Mandala Folk Dance Center

St. Paul's Presbyterian Church
1399 Forty-third Avenue
(415) 648-8489
www.themandala.org

Thursday, 7:30 P.M.

Have you been curious about folk dancing and seeking a venue to try it? This group, together since 1971, certainly bends toward the silver haired, but all are welcome. Know, however, that instruction only happens on Thursdays that are not the first or last of the month. Special events include on-site workshops and an occasional live band to keep things lively. Mandala also teaches a class on Sunday at Golden Gate Senior Center for those age fifty-five and over, where admission is just $1.

THE CATCH

Admission is generally $4.

Mission Cultural Center for Latino Arts

2868 Mission Street

(415) 821-1155

www.missionculturalcenter.org

While most public, drop-in dance classes are fairly affordable (in the range of $10 to $12), some highlights of the center's myriad dance classes are too good to pass up for the financially challenged. Many classes are offered for $8, such as Wednesday's Samba Jam for all ages. But do not overlook the many offerings of capoeira, fusion dance hip-hop, merengue, or rehearsal classes for the neighborhood's giant Carnival festival, all priced from about $2 to $4. Saturday has a good spread of classes for youths that feature dance but include some arts and crafts, each for just $2 to $4. And on Tuesday, Dance Azteca, a celebration in cultural movement for people of all ages, is absolutely free.

THE CATCH
Most classes cost from $2 to $12.
}

Pick School of Ballroom Dancing

380 Eighteenth Avenue

(415) 752-5658

www.pickdance.com

Sunday, 3:00 P.M.; Saturday, 9:00 P.M.

This elegant little school of dance offers both private and group courses and recommends a program of both for new students. Those looking to scuff their heels on the cheap can take advantage of some of the finer points of the open schedule. Both the Sunday and Saturday open floor practices listed above may not provide the individual attention that many students of ballroom dance seek, but they do provide over two hours of dressed-up fun on the floor for a paltry sum.

THE CATCH
Sunday practices are $5; Saturday $10.
}

Queer Jitterbugs

At Queer Ballroom

Live Art Gallery

151 Potrero Avenue

(415) 305-8242

www.queerjitterbugs.com/volunteer.htm

If you're lesbian, gay, bisexual, or transgendered (LGBT) and you simply cannot get enough of swing dancing, no partner and no experience are necessary to let your feet join the club. Best of all, if you agree to help with some of the legwork, such as hanging flyers, working the door, etc., you will qualify for free entry to weekly and special events, including the annual gala ball.

THE CATCH
Volunteer to qualify for free entry to events.

Rhythm and Motion Dance Center

1133 Mission Street
(415) 621-0643
www.rhythmandmotion.com

Ballet, fusion, hip-hop, salsa, and yoga: If it means moving your joints this way and that, then this popular studio—with a packed schedule of classes for adults, kids, and teens—has a competitively priced class with your name on it. Their philosophy is that no dancer should be left out, thus they offer a very flexible panoply of work-exchange programs ranging from one-time event volunteering to regular staff positions.

THE CATCH
Work-exchange programs are available.

KEEPING DANCERS ON THEIR TOES

When the clumsiness of the arts scene threatens to topple their best efforts, the local SF dance community falls into the arms of the Dancers' Group (3252A 19th Street; 415-920-9181; www.dancersgroup.org), a non-profit supported by a number of grants that keeps dance artists in the air. This organization provides monies for aspiring visionaries to take risk in the arts, nonprofit umbrella status to help smaller dance organizations secure funding, and emergency financial support to help support the lives of dancers stricken with AIDS or other life-threatening illnesses. In addition, this service for dancers produces a number of annual publications, helps promote large-scale dance events, and supports the growth and longevity of the community as a whole.

San Francisco Caper Cutters

St. Paul's Presbyterian Church
1399 Forty-third Avenue
(415) 751-3105
www.sfsquaredancing.org

Monday, 7:30 P.M.

Square dancing ain't just for squares, pardner, and this long-established group of mostly seniors has been do-si-do'ing here on the quiet for years. Note that four couples must be present to make a square, but that one can come stag and find a second half on premises. Most courses are for experienced dancers, but special beginners classes take place from time to time.

THE CATCH } It costs $5 to caper.

San Francisco Feldenkrais Community Clinic

At the Women's Building
(415) 431-1180, ext. 11

Every Tuesday except the fourth Tuesday of the month, 6:00 to 7:00 P.M.

THE CATCH } $5 to $10 donation requested, but no one is turned away for lack of funds.

Awareness Through Movement offers group classes in healthy movement for the general public, regardless of age or physical ability.

Shawl-Anderson Dance Company

2704 Alcatraz Avenue, Berkeley
(510) 654-5921
www.shawl-anderson.org

THE CATCH } Passes are only good for four weeks after purchase.

Most suckers will pay $12 per drop-in modern, jazz, and ballet class, but students able to shell out for a frequent-use pass can pay as little as $6.50. Classes are offered for both adults and kids.

Studio Gracia

19 Heron Street
(415) 307-4782
www.studiogracia.com

If one doesn't mind trading time cleaning or manning the front desk at this spacious SoMa studio, then the full schedule of classes in "dirty salsa," Brazilian samba, or Argentinean tango won't twirl the cash out of your pocket. Inquire within.

THE CATCH } Work-exchange programs available.

Sundance Saloon

Space550
550 Barneveld Avenue
www.sundancesaloon.org

Thursday, 6:30 P.M.; Sunday, 5:00 P.M.

Recently increased to twice weekly, this very popular LGBT event skews very heavily toward men only, but all are welcome. Two rooms feature lessons in multiple styles of two-step, West Coast swing, and other finer points of country-western

 dance, for a measly sum, with the real kitsch of country, like Dolly herself, piping off the DJ's tables. Boots, hats, and plaid are worn without irony, however. Thankfully, a full bar and coat check are available.

THE CATCH — $5 for lessons and all-night dancing.

Zaccho Studio

1777 Yosemite Avenue, Studio 330
(415) 822-6744
www.zaccho.org

Serving where the city's need may be greatest, in the often overlooked and arts-poor Bayview/Hunters Point District, Zaccho offers high-level, conceptual, mentally and physically challenging courses in movement and body performance for youths and adults.

THE CATCH — Classes are pay what you can afford, with $15 suggested.

{SECTION 2: LIVING}
IN SAN FRANCISCO

{FOOD: }
CHEAP EATS

"Earth provides enough to satisfy every man's need, but not every man's greed."

—*Mohandas K. Gandhi*

Few things taste better than the low-cost lunch that someone else has prepared, and those who claim that there's no such thing as a free lunch simply weren't trying hard enough. When pots of our own homemade lentil soup begin to leave the taste buds dull, we hardworking, easygoing eaters can find myriad ways to fill our bellies on the sly. While by no means a complete list, here are a few favorite opportunities to chow down on the cheap—and don't forget that a Ziploc-lined messenger bag can hold the beginnings of the next meal as well.

CHEAP FOOD-HEAVY HAPPY HOURS

(For booze-only happy hours, see pages 89–95.)

Andalu
3198 16th Street
(415) 621-2211
www.andalusf.com

Tuesday, 5:30 to 10:00 P.M.

This is not a happy hour per se, as the list of sixty wines by the glass is still priced regularly, most around $8. But what makes this evening special in this lovely, trendy, date-friendly environment, are the dollar ahi tuna tartar tacos with chili, lime, and mango salsa served fresh, plentifully, and all night long. If you were planning the beginnings of a night out on the town, this is a great way to save a few bucks on food to start things off.

THE CATCH You will very likely get a hairy eyeball if you order nothing but the tacos.

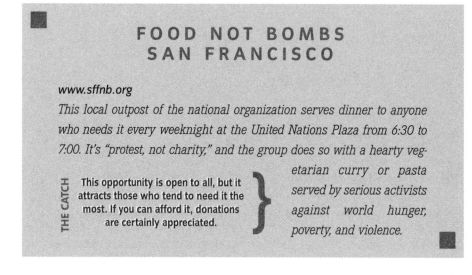

FOOD NOT BOMBS
SAN FRANCISCO

www.sffnb.org

This local outpost of the national organization serves dinner to anyone who needs it every weeknight at the United Nations Plaza from 6:30 to 7:00. It's "protest, not charity," and the group does so with a hearty veg-

THE CATCH
This opportunity is open to all, but it attracts those who tend to need it the most. If you can afford it, donations are certainly appreciated.

}

etarian curry or pasta served by serious activists against world hunger, poverty, and violence.

Bacar
448 Brannan Street
(415) 904-4100
www.bacarsf.com

Thursday, 4:00 to 6:30 P.M.; Friday, 2:30 to 6:30 P.M.

Few things make Downtown workers happier than the weekly Bacar happy hour, and for good reason: This elegant eatery opens its doors to the rest of us with half-off cocktails, half-off beer, a half-dozen varieties of excellent oysters for a buck a piece, and a generous cone of fries for just $6. The blackberry margarita is a hands-down favorite, but the other quality mixed drinks will surely satisfy any thirst for around $5. Note that this can draw a crowd, particularly on Friday. However, reservations for large groups are accepted, and there is additional, less visible seating at the bar downstairs.

Butterfly

Pier 33 at the Embarcadero
(415) 864-8999
www.butterflysf.com

Monday through Friday, 4:00 to 7:00 P.M.

Elegant white tablecloths, waterfront views, hordes of tourists, and an incredible daily nibbles and drinks menu cater to the palate of the secretively budget conscious. A mere five bucks buys the likes of duck confit spring rolls and ample plates of fried calamari, while beers are just $3. Or go nuts with your beverage budget and sample the Candied Ginger Collins, where gin meets ginger syrup and fresh lime, or the Cherry Blossom, where black cherry vodka mingles with lemon juice, sugar, and cranberry for $5. The bargain for what you see and get is one of the best on the bay.

Chaya San Francisco

132 the Embarcadero
(415) 777-8688
www.thechaya.com

Monday through Friday, 5:00 to 7:30 P.M.; Saturday, 5:00 to 10:00 P.M.; Sunday, 5:00 to 11:00 P.M.

Daily drink specials, including martinis, quality sake, and wines served fancy, hover at around $6, and numerous wickedly good and high-quality sushi rolls swing from $4 and up during this frequent reason to see and be seen along the Embarcadero. Admittedly, it's not the cheapest way to find sushi in the city, but for the quality and location, this is a fraction of what most diners pay here during prime time. Chaya offers a more traditional bar menu of beef tenderloin, quesadillas, and the like to please even the fish-hating among us.

City Tavern

3200 Fillmore Street
(415) 567-0918
www.citytavernsf.com

Tuesday, 3:00 to 10:00 P.M.; Monday and Wednesday through Friday, 3:00 to 7:00 P.M.

The Cow Hollow neighborhood simply buzzes with an eating and drinking frenzy, particularly on Tuesday, when an extensive menu of beers and food—good food, too, like turkey burgers, pizzas, chicken wings, and salads—is practically paying you to drink and eat them, priced at just $2 each.

THE CATCH
This well-known haunt for the hungry fills up rapidly, and no reservations are accepted. Prepare to get there early and get out quickly.

Frisson

244 Jackson Street
(415) 956-3004
www.frissonsf.com

Free drinks and food the first Thursday of the month, 7:00 to 9:00 P.M.; daily happy hour, 5:00 to 7:00 P.M.

As part of the unveiling of its new monthly art installation, the restaurant offers some complimentary snacks and drinks to help you, uh, see the art better in the lush, darker-than-dark funky lounge. This is a rare and golden opportunity to soak up the ambience of one of SF's most attractive restaurants for the low, low price of zilch. Plan it right and you can take it all in even longer. Every night during the after-work hours, a host of wonderful small plates, such as spring rolls and pork croquettes, are just $5, as are the exquisite house cocktails, such as the Le Long Frisson and the daily caipirinha. This is one of the best values in elegance around.

Hog Island Oyster Company

1 Ferry Building
(415) 391-7117
www.hogislandoysters.com

Monday and Thursday, 5:00 to 7:00 P.M.

Imagine this: It's after work and you're sitting outside the architecturally stunning Ferry Building with a view of the boats coming in, Angel Island, and Oakland across the water. That $3.50 pint of delicious, cold beer—Anchor Steam, Fat Tire, or whatever else is on tap—tastes cold and sweet and is the perfect foil for the outstandingly fresh and local oysters, briny, topped with a champagne vinegar mignonette or with just a dash of lemon and hot sauce. Either way, they only cost a buck a piece, and you're in hog heaven.

Kincaid's Bayhouse Restaurant

1 Franklin Street, #70, Oakland
(510) 835-8600
www.jacksbistro.com

Monday through Thursday, 4:00 to 6:00 P.M.

It's worth crossing the East Bay for this waterside gem's lovely views and on-vacation factor. The real draw, of course, is an early-dinner experience that will leave your wallet flush with enough cash to cross the bridge home. Just $2.99 buys a draft beer, a glass of chardonnay, or a made-from-scratch margarita (the clear choice). The appetizer menu has a plethora of selections that are half off, including grilled meat skewers, crab cakes, ribs, seared fish, and more—all tiny plates at a bargain rate of about four bucks each.

The Lion Pub

2062 Divisadero Street
(415) 567-6565

Tuesday through Saturday, 9:00 to 10:00 P.M.

These aren't exactly the most dependable bar snacks offered, but if you hit it here at the right time, the generosity makes it worth the gamble. In addition to an excellent spread of cheese, crackers, lunch meat, and crudités, sometimes sushi, smoked salmon, and chips and dips are offered as well. While you're awaiting the grub, take in the time-warp nature of the ambience—heavy wooden chairs, brass, dark decor, and fireplaces that come together to create the feel of a forgotten airport holding station. Note that there is no sign out front stating the name of the bar.

Madrone Lounge

500 Divisadero Street
(415) 241-0202
www.madronelounge.com

Free pizza on Sunday, 6:00 to 8:00 P.M.; daily happy hour, 6:00 to 9:00 P.M.

The purchase of a single drink is your ticket to free pizza slices that help you nurse that weekend hangover and transition back into workweek mode. In the background, vintage television shows help you forget, but the free band that starts at 8:00 P.M. should jab those neurons into firing once again. Just to make sure you don't feel the financial pinch, the early bird gets this worm: $2 Bud tall boys, $3 wells, $4 mojitos or infused vodka. Extraspecial bonus: It's also industry night for those who work in the field of bars, restaurants, and nightclubs. For your service to the community, you can purchase half-price drinks all night. What a deal!

New Delhi Restaurant

160 Ellis Street
(415) 397-8470
www.newdelhirestaurant.com

Monday through Saturday, 4:00 to 6:00 P.M. and 10:00 P.M. to midnight

Inside and outside of the dinner hour, this popular restaurant and drinking establishment lays it all out—samosas, pakoras, and tandori chicken drumsticks, that is. The food is good, but positively ambrosia, considering it's a free serve-yourself appetizer bar. They make their money from the drinks you'll buy—$3 beers, house wine, and well drinks. No matter how you slice it, this is a bargain good enough to get on the regular rotation.

TEN GREAT, NO FRILLS
EATERIES FOR UNDER $10

Good Luck Dim Sum
736 Clement Street
(415) 386-3388

Nearly any dim sum joint along this stretch of Clement will fill the gullet, but this is one of the better choices. With three of these and four of those, two people can eat for well under $10.

Il Pollaio
555 Columbus Avenue
(415) 362-7727

It's tough to eat in North Beach for less than a Jackson note, but these finger-lickin' chicken, soups, and awesome side salad full meals are worth taking under your wing.

In-n-Out Burger
333 Jefferson Street

Normally fast food is fast food. But this is gourmet accelerated dining with a cult following and one of the few inexpensive and reliable eateries in the very touristed Fisherman's Wharf.

La Taqueria
2889 Mission Street
(415) 285-7117

Every San Franciscan has a favorite taco and burrito joint, and sometimes that favorite can change by the day. But they all share one thing in common: heaps of food, dirt cheap, to fill you up for hours. This is one of the most authentic, freshest, and most popular.

Lucca Ravioli Company
1100 Valencia Street
(415) 647-5581

There's no place to sit down at this awesome Italian market, but a half sheet of the house-made Sicilian-style pizza for five bucks is a slice of cheapskate heaven and can easily feed three or four.

Manora's Thai Cuisine Restaurant
1600 Folsom Street
(415) 861-6224
www.manorathai.com

Bring your appetite. The lunch combination is a cup of soup, two items from the menu of over a dozen dishes, plus fried rice, served up for about $8. Smaller appetites can munch a ton of dishes for just $6.

Pakwan
653 Clay Street; (415) 834-9904

501 O'Farrell Street; (415) 776-0160

3182 16th Street; (415) 255-2440

Self-service Pakistani food that's robustly flavorful and cheap, with many curries around $5. Add nan for $1 and bryani rice for $2.

Papa Toby's Revolution Cafe
3248 22nd Street
(415) 642-0474

San Francisco is blessed with a number of coffee shops serving good food that can always deliver a soup, salad, or sandwich to do the job. This one is one of your better choices, with consistently fresh ingredients and good vibes.

Tuk Tuk Thai and Asian Market
1581 University Avenue, Berkeley
(510) 666-1125

The easygoing deli is well worth a stop if you need enough food to feed all of Bangkok. Three excellent dishes, such as pad Thai, chicken with basil and chili, and beef noodles, plus rice, are just $7.

Tu Lan
8 6th Street
(415) 626-0927

Don't let the Tenderloin location scare you off. This is excellent, freshly prepared Vietnamese food that's fast, cheap, and out of control.

Ponzu

401 Taylor Street
(415) 775-9997
www.ponzurestaurant.com

Monday through Friday, 4:30 to 7:00 P.M.

The AtoZen Happy Hour is a great way to dissolve your workday at the bottom of a White Tiger (sake, Cointreau, lime juice, and salt) or a Tuk-Tuk (Gray Goose orange vodka, peach schnapps, cranberry, Thai basil, fresh lime). Best of all, several tasty dim sum bites, such as steamed pork dumplings or Chinese five-spice meatballs, are just fifty cents a bite.

Restaurant Seven Fifty at the Hilton San Francisco Financial District

750 Kearny Street
(415) 433-6600
www.sanfranciscohiltonhotel.com

Monday through Friday, 2:00 to 7:00 P.M.

They say Financial District, I say Chinatown, but we all agree that a bargain is a bargain. And while the drink specials change both daily and seasonally—plan on a fancy-schmancy hotel cocktail for about $6—the real cheap eats here are the food, where the menu of filling pub grub appetizers are half off and, coincidentally, the deal actually happens at a time when you would actually *want* to eat dinner. You can easily make a meal of the likes of jalapeño poppers, chicken nachos, garlic fries, mussels, and buffalo wings for about five bucks a generous plate.

Scott Howard

500 Jackson Street
(415) 956-7040
www.scotthowardsf.com

Monday through Friday, 5:00 to 6:00 P.M.

Literally happening in a single hour, you may have to bring your own happy to truly get your money's worth. But in an attempt to make this excellent eatery a drinkery as well, Scott Howard is testing the spirited waters by offering the normally $10 top-shelf creative libations for a mere $7 (agreed, that's not exactly a giveaway), plus the requisite oysters for just a buck. It's worth a splurge to sample some of the bar's most creative efforts, such as the Cotton Tail (a whirl of Hendricks vodka, carrot juice, toasted cumin, and smoked Spanish salt) or the Dragon Slayer (made from St. George's whiskey, Qi Tea liqueur, blood orange syrup, and brandied cherries).

Shima Sushi

601 Van Ness Avenue

(415) 292-9997

Monday through Thursday, 7:30 to 9:30 P.M.

Normally, cheap sushi is something to be avoided, but centrally situated Opera Plaza is home to this decent-enough sushi spot that really hits it home for a late-night postmovie bite. Large hot sakes and a menu of handrolls are just three bucks a pop during those magical two hours of low-cost bliss. Take that, roll it, and eat it.

LOW-COST FOOD STORES AND FARMERS' MARKETS

Alemany Farmers' Market

100 Alemany Boulevard (at Interstate 280)

(415) 647-2043

Saturday, 6:00 A.M. to 3:00 P.M.

About a million reasons exist to support your local farmers' market—the environmental benefits of local produce; the advance of a local economy; healthier, better-tasting food, etc. But we penny-pinchers know that all of this is a great mission—provided we can get our tomatoes and melons at a good price. The Bay Area is guilty of elevating the humble weekend produce market to Mount Olympus status, and the resulting $6 a pound for nearly anything is just too much dough. This is one of the few regular fruit and vegetable parades that boasts old farm-stand prices, great variety, and still supports the mission that makes waking up at the wee hours on a Saturday a reasonable request.

Bargain Bank

599 Clement Street; (415) 221-4852

566 Minnesota Street; (415) 552-7283

1541 Polk Street; (415) 345-1623

www.bargainbank.com

Though they used to sell all sorts of personal care items and sundries for the home, now the inventory is almost exclusively dry-packaged gourmet food from around the world, plus heaps of priced-to-move wine (seriously—like $3 a bottle) and other beverages. Ninety-nine cents can easily buy you a box of cereal, a bottle of marinade or salad dressing, some imported fancy cookies, and the like, making this a worthy stop when party planning.

TIP The warehouse location on Minnesota and 18th Streets has a wine-tasting license, and you try samples of most of the stock while you shop.

Bayview Hunters Point Farmers' Market

3rd and Galvez Streets

(415) 355-3723

Saturday, 9:30 A.M. to 1:30 P.M., May through December only

This is another gem on the fresh and local produce circuit, where $10 can buy as much as you can comfortably eat in a week, most of which was grown by minority farmers to boot. It's a small market, but certainly worth a visit on a weekend during the season. Even luxury items, like blackberries and raspberries, are sold at some of the best prices anywhere in the city.

Grocery Outlet

2001 Fourth Street, Berkeley; (510) 666-0670

2900 Broadway, Oakland; (510) 465-5649

www.groceryoutlets.com

This left-coast chain began in San Francisco in the 1940s, and its commitment to "bargain only" food and household items is still going strong. They buy bulk over-stocked or bulk stocked goods and sell them at significant discount—everything from frozen egg rolls to Australian wine to hand soap and all that you can imagine in between, depending on the market at the moment. You never know what you're going to find, but there will be plenty of it, and it will be cheap.

L & M Produce Market

2169 Mission Street

(415) 864-1330

In truth, any produce market along Mission between 16th and 24th Streets is going to save you a bundle, but this is one of our favorites for reliability, freshness, selection, and a helpful staff. You'll find an excellent selection of the Latino grocery items that the neighborhood mandates (think fresh cactus, tamarind, dried chili peppers, and canned Mexican cooking sauces). They also have a great selection of Thai items, like fresh coconut, noodles, and curry pastes, for a fraction of the price of the big chains.

New May Wah Supermarket

547 Clement Street

(415) 668-2583

In addition to a dizzying array of superfresh fish, meat, fruits, and vegetables at third-world prices, this outstanding and mammoth Chinese grocery supercenter has all of the usual specimens that make shopping for food in another country interesting—pickled burdock, turtles on ice, and more dried fungi than you can shake a Pocky Stick at. Even if you're not a gourmet Chinese chef, there is enough here that's priced well enough to keep you coming back for the savings—no coupons required.

Rainbow Grocery Cooperative

1745 Folsom Street

(415) 863-0620

www.rainbowgrocery.org

Rainbow has a lot going for it—organic produce, worker-owned labor policies, and a sharp, liberal, political edge. But when it comes to saving money, the enormous serve-yourself, bulk-bin aisles are a great place to get just the right amount of dried cranberry beans, amaranth flour, nutritional yeast, trail mix, Japanese pickled plums, or about a zillion other items that you need, without paying for anything extra (or using a boatload of packaging). Extra change stays in your pocket if you bring your own bags, plastic containers, and bottles in which to carry it all home.

The SHARE Food Network

This organization distributes high-quality, affordable nutritious food as a way to build community and strengthen families. For $16 plus two hours of volunteer service, anyone may receive a SHARE package full of fresh vegetables, fruits, staple items, and frozen meats. The same amount of food would cost approximately $35 to $40 at the supermarket. There are several locations that distribute SHARE food boxes; call the United Way's HELPLINK at (415) 772-4357 (HELP) for a location near you.

Sunset Supermarket

2425 Irving Street

(415) 566-6504

If mammoth local grocery store Safeway sold Asian goods and cut its prices by about two thirds, you would have this massive food-shopping mecca's expansive size and depth. All items around the perimeter—fresh deli food, meat, fish, fruits, veg, and, yes, even some dairy—are priced way below what you'd pay at any comparable store. Even the canned goods, packaged foods, and beverages—some familiar, many worth exploring—certainly offer you enough savings to make this destination worth a trip.

Trader Joe's

401 Bay Street; (415) 351-1013

3 Masonic Avenue; (415) 346-9964

555 9th Street; (415) 863-1292

You hate it because it's a national chain, you love it because it has outstanding organic pizza for just four bucks—either way, you're here all the time, and there's a $50 admission fee, redeemable for jarred pesto, imported chocolate, and inexpensive olive oil every time you walk in the door (well, OK, we exaggerate, but you get the idea). Parking is often a nightmare, but once you get inside, this is a dream filled with gourmet goodies, snack foods, sweets, and household items that are excellent buys, and most are outstanding quality.

NOTABLE BARGAIN BUFFETS— ALL YOU CARE TO STUFF DOWN YOUR THROAT FOR CHEAP

Goat Hill Pizza
300 Connecticut Street
(415) 641-1440
www.goathillpizza.com
Monday, 5:00 to 10:00 P.M.

All the pizza and salad you can ingest for $9.95 is wheeled around on carts like dim sum, hot and with a cornmeal crust. Kids ages six to twelve eat for just $6.

Helmand Restaurant
430 Broadway
(415) 362-0641
Tuesday through Friday, 11:30 A.M. to 2:30 P.M.

Sweetened fried pumpkin, lamb kebab in herbed yogurt sauce, soup, salad, and about a dozen other items fill this unusual (and plentiful) lunchtime offering of Afghani cuisine, all for $9.95.

India Clay Oven
2436 Clement Street
(415) 751-0505
http://indiaclayoven.com
Daily, 11:30 A.M. to 2:30 P.M.

Lunchtime lights up at this entirely huge selection of chicken, lamb, fish, and vegetarian Indian specialties for $7.95.

Poetry and Pizza

At Escape from New York Pizza
333 Bush Street
http://popizza.white.prohosting.com

First Friday of the month, 7:30 P.M.

Poetry, like sex and pizza, can be either great or just pretty good. Two out of three are served up here in abundance, with local poets knocking out verses while you knock back slices. At this stuff-yourself-silly pizza fest, your $5 "donation" goes toward a different local charity each month. True, you don't "have" to pay, but expect askance glances and attitude if you don't.

Raja Cuisine of India

500 Haight Street
(415) 255-6000
www.rajasf.com

Daily, 11:00 A.M. to 2:00 P.M.

Service can be curt and brusque, but hey, it's a buffet, it's cheap ($7.99), and you're mostly just serving yourself anyway. This is one of the few Indian eateries that regularly features tandori pizza.

Star of India

2127 Polk Street
(415) 292-6699
starofindiaonpolk.com

Daily

Nine dollars (technically, $8.95) is decent at lunch but a total giveaway during the dinner hour. The menu changes daily, but there is always a curry and all the accompaniments to suit every palate.

Tonga Room

950 Mason Street
(415) 772-5278
www.tongaroom.com

Monday through Friday, 5:00 to 7:00 P.M.

Technically this is a happy hour, and there is a one-drink Hawaiian cocktail minimum. But the $7 dinner-hour buffet is too large to be ignored, erupting with spare ribs, vegetable chow mein, pork buns, pot stickers, and the like. Not for the faint of grease.

THE GREAT SEE'S CANDY GIVEAWAY

Step into any See's Candy (www.sees.com)—there are seven city locations alone, plus the airport in San Francisco—and buy any single item and you will, almost always, be given an extra piece of chocolate confection with your purchase. Of course it's not going to be a pricey nut cluster; more often than not it's a butter cream or a fruit jelly something or other. But hey, it's free, and if you're paying for one piece, you suddenly have twice as much chocolate than you'd bargained for. And that's a very sweet deal indeed.

DINING ON A DIME— BARGAIN EATING IN NICE PLACES

Alamo Square Seafood Grill

803 Fillmore Street
(415) 440-2828

Sunday through Thursday, all day; Friday and Saturday, 5:30 to 6:30 P.M.

This cute, cozy, often overlooked seafood house on an unassuming stretch of Fillmore is a great bargain just ready for the reeling. The three-course prix fixe is $12.50. Guests have their choice of soup or salad and then receive the chef's choice of entrees—usually a seared piece of whatever recently had been swimming, prepared simply. The finale is a slab of a house-made dessert. These are top-feeding delights at bottom-feeder prices.

THE CATCH: Service can move at subglacial speeds; don't expect to flow in and out quickly.

Chapeau!

1408 Clement Street
(415) 750-9787

Sunday through Thursday, 5:00 to 6:00 P.M.

Delectably French, deceptively elegant, this is a classy spot for European dining, and if your butt can get in the chair before the dinner rush, you can have it all at a tremendous value: a three-course prix fixe dinner for $19. Diners tip their hat to onion soup baked with crouton and Emmental, roasted pork loin with French green lentils and caramelized apples, and vividly memorable classic French profiteroles. Served with precision and professionalism from a deeply caring husband-and-wife team, this is an affordable elegant evening meal at about two-thirds the usual cost.

The City Dish

www.sfcitydish.com

Kevin Blum is your host to this weekly e-mail list serving outstanding and ever-changing restaurant deals. Get on the inside track for free appetizers, buy-one-get-one-free offers, cheap drinks, and more from good places that he can cajole into a group discount. Best of all, it costs nothing to get on the mailing list, and there's no coupons to tote. For nearly every offer, just say you saw it on the City Dish. Ka-ching!

Dine About Town

www.dineabouttown.com

January

The San Francisco Convention and Visitors Bureau is always striving to keep SF's elite culinary houses on the menu. During this long, cold, postholiday month, when restaurant business is traditionally slow, the CVB convinces one hundred or so of the town's favorite high-class eateries to compose special three-course prix fixe menus. For $21.95 at lunch and $31.95 at dinner, pinkie-out, penny-pinching eaters can get some real bang for their buck, particularly when you consider that many participating restaurants sell a single entree for about the same price. If you've always wanted to try Rubicon or the Acme Chophouse, this is one of the most affordable ways to dig in.

Firewood Cafe

4248 18th Street
(415) 252-0999
www.firewoodcafe.com

Tuesday

Rotisserie chicken, mammoth salads, wood-fired pizza, and homemade pastas are good enough and under $10 or so every day, but each Tuesday lunch or dinner patrons can knock 20 percent off of their total bill, no matter what. Wines for five bucks a glass and a good kids' menu should position this cafe on the roster of every cheapskate's regular dinner rotation.

Home

2100 Market Street
(415) 503-0333
www.home-sf.com

Daily, 5:00 to 6:00 P.M.

You'd be hard pressed to find a better early-bird dining value anywhere else in the city—three courses for $10.99. As if three generous courses of hardcore comfort food weren't enough to feed the Castro dweller's heart and stomach, the restaurant throws in a glass of house wine for good measure. There are rules, however. Diners must *absolutely* be seated and ordering before 6:00, so no blowing in at the last minute. And the menu is always chef's choice, be it cauliflower soup, a pulled pork sandwich, and strawberry rhubarb crisp, or iceberg wedge, meat loaf, and sorbet.

THE CATCH No substitutions are allowed. }

Job Corps Advanced Culinary Academy Fine Dining Restaurant

Building 368, Ninth Street and Avenue C, Treasure Island
(415) 277-2370

Tuesday through Thursday, noon seating only

If you're willing to be the subject of some academic study, this is one of the most delicious ways to do it that we can think of. Advanced students of this Job Corps program are being trained to work as cooks and servers in restaurants and the hospitality industry, and they need diners to complete their experience. For about $12 ($3 starters, $6 entrees, and $3 desserts), those with time to lunch on beautiful Treasure Island will have the booty of a white-tablecloth dining experience for a song. The preparation of the food is a learning experience as well, but it almost always ranges from pretty good to excellent. The bargain, however, is consistently sublime.

THE CATCH Reservations are strongly encouraged. }

Millennium Restaurant

580 Geary Street

(415) 345-3900

www.millenniumrestaurant.com

Convert a Carnivore Night: second Wednesday of the month

It's a genius scheme, really. Vegetarians and vegans are asked to bring their flesh-eating friends in for dinner one night a month to feed them the likes of porcini and Anasazi bean posole with quinoa sweet potato cake, pumpkin seed emulsion, and avocado-jicama relish, and then ask the carnivores to see the light of the meat-free diet—all for 25 percent off the total food bill (entrees are usually around $20). Certainly if every meal were as tasty as that of chef Eric Tucker's, none of us would touch meat again. No matter how you stand, this exquisite, elegant, and award-winning dining destination dangles a financial incentive to get the doubting in to give it a try, and the whole table can benefit from the experience.

THE CATCH } The discount does not apply to alcohol.

2223 Market Restaurant

2223 Market Street

(415) 431-0692

www.2223restaurant.com

Tuesday

Whereas most entrees run upward of $20 at this well-healed Castro eatery, one night a week the tie knot loosens, and a special menu features all entrees for just $12 and starters for $6. Yum out to the likes of achiote pork loin with queso fresco papusa, black bean chili, and fried plantains, or southern fried chicken nestled next to smashed buttermilk potatoes and slaw. The menu changes seasonally, emphasizes what's fresh and local, supports sustainably farmed ingredients, and uses hormone- and antibiotic-free protein sources—yet more reasons to feel good about eating here and saving a few bucks.

Zazie

941 Cole Street

(415) 564-5332

www.zaziesf.com

If you're splurging, this is a great little neighborhood French place to do it in, and you needn't be an early bird for a bite of this worm. A three-course dinner is $19.50. Cozy, home-style cooking like mussels in white wine and garlic, followed by fish soup Provençal, and finished with crème brûlée—it's a delicious side stuffer (and a great way to plump up your date). The best part is that this special is available all night, every evening—a rarity in low-priced fine dining.

{ WINE, BEER, AND SPIRITS: }
THE LOW-HANGING FRUIT

"Nature provides a free lunch, but
only if we control our appetites."
—William Ruckelshaus

If we learned nothing else in college, it's that free booze is the best booze, with the cleanest flavor and the most lingering effects. Some of us may be charming enough to have a cocktail or two purchased for us, but that's an unreliable strategy, often leading to the nasty side effect of forced conversation with guys in mullets and stained flannel. Remain charming when in a bar-type atmosphere, but keep this toolbox of free and low-cost beverage opportunities up your sleeve. At these prices, you can even appease your whining friend and afford to be the one chiming in on the next round. Or not. Either way, the spirit of a cocktail poured on your behalf shall move you.

Anchor Brewing Company Tour

1705 Mariposa Street
(415) 863-8350
www.anchorbrewing.com/about_us/tourinfo.htm

The only thing better than seeing how San Francisco's favorite beer is made is the generous free tasting of the Anchor family of beer products that follows at the end. A totally unique, delicious, and refreshing SF beer-related experience, from grain to wert to bottle, this is a great way to learn a bit of the city's history through hops. Children are welcome on the free tour, though tasting is available only to an age-appropriate audience. Tours fill up months in advance and are offered once daily, so book far ahead to ensure there's a tasting glass with your name on it.

THE CATCH: Reservations far in advance are absolutely required.

The Attic

3336 24th Street
(415) 643-3376

Daily happy hour, 5:00 to 7:30 P.M.

A mere $2.50 will buy you a draft beer, a well martini (if you dare), or a well manhattan or cosmopolitan. And while it might not be the most nutritionally sound choice, you would not be the first to eat nothing but the overflowing bowls of Goldfish crackers for dinner. It's dark enough in here, however, to pretend that you're someplace more divey or more posh, depending on your perspective. . . .

Blur

1121 Polk Street
(415) 567-1918

Weekdays, 4:00 to 6:00 P.M.

Oh, pay ye shall for these fancy house libations—ten bucks or more for crazy con-
coctions like the Blurry Dog—vodka, sake, and grapefruit juice poured strong
enough to fulfill the bar's namesake. And how does this affect you? In the early-
evening hours Blur offers the entire bar menu of tipplers at two drinks for the
price of just one. Bring a friend and you'll look like a big spender.

Dalva

3121 16th Street
(415) 252-7740

Daily happy hour, 4:00 to 7:00 P.M.

The after-work/after-class crowd would agree: Domestic beer, house-made sangria,
and well drinks for under three bones is a total steal, particularly when it positions
you nearby so many cheap taquerias for dinner. This is a neighborhood favorite,
and these early-evening hours make it an affordable way to entertain even the
cheapest drunk.

Destino

1815 Market Street
(415) 552-4451
www.destinosf.com

Monday through Thursday, 5:00 to 7:00 P.M.

Two-for-one mojitos—and these are goooood mojitos, too. Fresh mint, muddled to
aromatic death, with the right balance of sugar, booze, and bubble. This tiny,
stylish, often overlooked Castro joint knows how to pour 'em, and during these
choice hours, they're all yours at bargain prices.

THE CATCH   This is mostly a restaurant, with less than ten seats at the bar (the
only place a tightwad can logically sit without ordering food).
Prepare to arrive early, stand with a drink in your hand, or possibly
fight the midweek cocktail-loving crowd.

540 Club
540 Clement Street
(415) 752-7276
www.540-club.com

Daily happy hour, 4:00 to 7:00 P.M.

In addition to the daily early-evening happy hour, there are two nights that are tough to ignore at this out-of-the-way Richmond District haunt. Monday night features $1 well drinks from 10:00 to midnight, and on Tuesday, during the same prime-time slot, one pays just $2 for martinis, lemon drops, manhattans, and the like. Sign on to the mailing list via the Web site and you'll be in the know when it's free taco night or trivia night with prizes, and you'll hear about other great events at this comfy, fun, and hip hangout.

Holy Cow
1535 Folsom Street
(415) 621-6087
www.theholycow.com

Never having to pay a cover charge is a very good thing. Some say that a room brimming with top-40 hits and Stepford-looking blonde women "slumming" in the Big City on a weekend is also a good thing. Neither one should be taken for granted. But what is pure holy gospel is that the shortest path between you and a cocktail is the cheap one, and here no tightwad will be disappointed. Thursday features dollar wells and Buds from 9:00 to 11:30 P.M. Friday features half-priced drinks for just one golden hour—9:00 to 10:00 P.M. Saturday offers the same deal, along with some potent $3 specialty house cocktail.

Home Restaurant
2032 Union Street
(415) 931.5006
www.home-sf.com

Daily, 4:00 to 8:00 P.M.

While the Castro location of Home is the place for a well-priced meal, its cousin in the north of the city on Union Street has more of a sports bar and drinking vibe, and as such, it's a great place to kick off an early evening and keep a few dollars in your pocket (no easy feat in this neighborhood). Two-for-one drinks are offered daily from 4:00 to 8:00 P.M. And while the same mac-n-cheese and banana pudding is on both Home menus, the bar here is a separate entity, so the thirsty are most welcome without the need to order food.

WINE COUNTRY
WINE-TASTING ROOMS
WITH FREE TASTINGS

The only drawback in going wine tasting in Napa and Sonoma Counties is the need to drive home after being sloshed with a good amount of delicious, robust zinfandels and gewürztraminers. The positive aspects deeply weight the scale, and this is a quintessential way to spend a Northern California afternoon just an hour or so north of San Francisco. True penny-pinchers will want to bring along their own bottled water, bread, cheese, and fruit (and in summer, add a hat and some serious sunscreen to that list). Many places charge just a few dollars for tastings, and most will allow you to apply that money to purchases. But if you're looking to taste the sweetest, freest fruit on the vine, here is a listing of those that will allow you to taste for nothing, and you won't even have to mash grapes for the privilege. Note that most wineries in Napa have a bigger name and a bigger tourist draw, hence they are more likely to charge for the privilege of the taste. Avoiding the crowds also means avoiding the $3 to $10 "glass" fees of the larger vineyards.

Alexander Valley Vineyards, *8644 Highway 128, Healdsburg; (707) 433-7209; www.avvwine.com*

Cline Cellars, *24737 Arnold Drive (Highway 121), Sonoma; (707) 940-4030, (800) 546-2070; www.clinecellars.com*

Field Stone Winery, *10075 Highway 128, Healdsburg; (707) 433-7266; www.fieldstonewinery.com*

Fritz Winery, *24691 Dutcher Creek Road, Cloverdale; (707) 894-3389; www.fritzwinery.com*

Frog's Leap, *8815 Conn Creek Road, Rutherford; (800) 959-4704; www.frogsleap.com*

Hop Kiln Winery, *6050 Westside Road, Healdsburg; (707) 433-6491; www.hopkilnwinery.com*

And for Free Snacks . . .

Sonoma Cheese Factory
2 Spain Street, Sonoma
(707) 996-1931
www.sonomajack.com

Situated right on the main artery of beautiful Sonoma Square, this is one of the best (and least expensive) places to pick up picnic supplies in a convenient locale—tote a blanket and you can even have your picnic right here in the park. However, visitors are cordially invited to try before they buy, and while the cheese samples of various flavors of Monterey Jack are tiny, they are plentiful, savory, filling, and unmonitored. Have your fill of pepper Jack and pesto Jack and dozens more before buying a thing. You might only require the bread, wine, and sausage when you're through.

Viansa Winery and Italian Marketplace
25200 Arnold Drive, Sonoma
(707) 935-4700
www.viansa.com

Here you can dip pretzels in more varieties of mustard than you can shake an olive-tapenade-covered-cracker at. The wine is so-so, but the jars of Cal-Med snack tastes—jams, chocolate sauces, condiments as interesting and as diverse as the terroir—are worth a stop for lining the gullet on your way to taste wine for the day.

Pacific Cafe

7000 Geary Boulevard

(415) 387-7091

Fresh, comfortable, unfussy seafood dishes are priced well and include soup or salad and a starter—but the no-reservations policy wins its way to the cheapskate's heart through the liver: free wine while you wait. The low-rent white wine flows fast and furious when the line gets going, which is nearly anytime around a mealtime. The longer you wait, the less you'll care you're waiting.

Pyramid Alehouse, Brewery, and Restaurant Tours

901 Gilman Street, Berkeley

(510) 528-9880

www.pyramidbrew.com

Monday through Friday, 5:30 P.M.; Saturday and Sunday, 2:00 and 4:00 P.M.

The Berkeley alehouse of this popular Seattle label offers free, drop-in tours and information on its brewery, plenty of time for question and answers, and other communications outreach ploys for the public. They are fully aware, however, that nothing says lovin' like something fresh from the tap, so every hourlong walkthrough and how-to has the follow-through of sweet, delicious, free beer. Those under age twenty-one will enjoy the soda samplings of the house brand, Thomas Kemper.

San Francisco Brewing Company

155 Columbus Avenue

(415) 434-3344

www.sfbrewing.com

Daily, 4:00 to 6:00 P.M. and midnight to 1:00 A.M.

The early bird will certainly chirp with glee and catch this worm in abundance: $1.75 pints. These daily dirt-cheap happy hours for fresh, locally made brew are an incredible bargain, particularly if you can score one of the coveted outdoor tables overlooking the comings and goings of the heart of North Beach. If a whole pint is too much to stomach, ten-ounce pours are available for just a buck.

San Francisco's My Open Bar

http://sf.myopenbar.com.

Get on the mailing list of this week's happenings that involve free booze, and buy the editors a cheap drink for all their efforts, will ya? This is a great, free resource to stay in the loop of the ever-evolving scene of dirt-cheap drinks and the occasional happy hour snack. When you're on the road, this Web site offers a where's-what in low-cost libations for New York and Los Angeles, too. Cleverly written, often updated, and wise beyond its years, all you have to do is tolerate a few ads for the most recent good word. Cheers to that!

St. George Spirits/Hangar One Tasting Room
2601 Monarch Street (at Alameda Point), Alameda
(510) 769-1601
www.stgeorgespirits.com

Visiting our local distillery of single malt whiskey, the popular Hangar One vodka, and eclectic Aqua Perfecta eau de vie concentrated liquors in wild flavors is worth the $10 splurge, when you consider that it's a whole afternoon of fun and about four shots of booze. Call to check the seasonal tasting room hours. Enhance the enjoyment of the great nautical outdoors by taking the Alameda Ferry from the SF Ferry Building, learn about the process of distilling fine spirits, and taste away.

Takara Sake
708 Addison Street, Berkeley
(510) 540-8250
www.takarasake.com

Daily, noon to 6:00 P.M.

The floors are recycled lumber, the tile is composed of recycled bottles, and the look of this massive space is more gallery than brewery. No matter how you slice it, this elegant environment is still paying out with free sake samples and a bit of information on how this rice wine has been brewed for thousands of year. Note that there is also a sake museum on-site; you are free to tour it while you swirl the contents of your glass.

The Toranado Pub
47 Haight Street
(415) 863.2276
www.toronado.com

Daily, 11:30 A.M. to 6:00 P.M.

This bar has many great things going for it: a tremendous beer selection of dozens of the best brews made anywhere in the world, for one. A great, laid-back, Haight locale, for two. And for low-rent drinkers with time on their hands, a daily $2.50 pint special that not only starts in the A.M. but also lasts for hours and hours and is a tremendous bargain when you factor in the quality. Sure, there are pints of PBR to be had for cheaper. But when you crave a real beer from Ireland, Germany, or Seattle, this is a hop-lover's hitching post.

{ SPA SERVICES,
HAIR CARE, AND MASSAGE:
F R E E   S T Y L E }

"Cannot people realize how large
an income is thrift?"

—*Marcus Tullius Cicero*

It's amazing how many hair salons, spas, and massage and bodywork centers have a hoity-toity British accent, sometimes even a fake one, on their outgoing voice mail. Why? Because the world of beauty and physical maintenance has come to be seen as an element of the rich and famous, an indulgence, a high-class and often high-priced affair. But as we tightwads can attest, the latter qualification need not always be the case. Grooming and personal hygiene needn't touch your pocketbook more than skin deep. If you know where to look and have some flexibility with your schedule and your desired results, many fine local professionals can keep you looking stunning without the sting of what most are shelling out for that fresh-from-the-spa glow. Dig deep, dive in, and get more thrive for your dime.

HAIR, BEAUTY, AND SPA SERVICES

Alexander G.
3115 Clement Street
(415) 876-4688
www.alexanderg.com

Exact policies are pretty amorphous, but interested individuals can sign up for the models list for some kind of hair style change, either a few weeks or a few months in the future, depending on your hair type, what kind of cut you'd like to have, and the type of demonstration the salon would like to perform.

THE CATCH

Cuts cost no more than $20.

Bayview Barber College

4912 3rd Street
(415) 822-3300
www.bayviewbarbercollege.com

Priding itself on turning out students of great skill and high moral standard, this learning institution schools its graduates in the arts of cutting hair, scalp treatments, hair relaxing, weaves, and other tools helpful to the African-American neighborhood that it educates and serves.

THE CATCH
Cuts are $6
($5 for seniors).
}

Beauty Bar

2299 Mission Street
(415) 285-0323
www.beautybar.com

Thursday through Saturday, 7:30 P.M. to midnight

This West Coast outpost of the national bar chain has a shtick that works: free, drunken nail care amidst kitschy strong cocktails. Simply order the mysteriously green Prell, the deceptively undumb Platinum Blonde, or any of the house specialties, sip away, and some chick will file your daggers and slap on a coat of polish. Don't expect the greatest 'cure of your life, mind you, as you're just a part of the ambience and scenery. However, for a night out with the girls where you'd planned to booze it up anyhoo, it's better than going home with that chipped black polish you came in with.

THE CATCH
You need a $10 drink purchase to snag the freebie.
}

Blade Runners Hair Studio

1792 Haight Street
(415) 751-1723
bladerunnershairstudio.com

Monday

Apprentice stylists need heads to roll around, and if you call and leave your name, phone number, and hair type, they will decide if and when they're going to roll with yours. This Upper Haight salon is usually quite chic, with a reputation for excellence, and this weekly discount styling can be a great way to let its ambience rub off on you for a fraction of the regular cost.

THE CATCH
Haircuts cost $15, color $30.
}

Carleton Hair International

865 Market, Suite C28A, San Francisco Center
(415) 495-8300

Monday and Thursday, 11:00 A.M.

Call the salon anytime to sign up for these seriously cut-rate services from experienced stylists in a posh setting—$20 haircut, color starting at $25. Most weeks, they do two learning sessions for which they need volunteer, hair-growing heads to practice new looks and techniques.

THE CATCH Haircuts cost $20, color starts at $25

Cinta Salon

23 Grant Avenue, #2
(415) 989-1000

Ten-dollar haircuts, or $20 for a color and $35 for highlights, based on current need. Don't expect to just call up and make an appointment when you want it, but applicants looking to add a little sizzle to their look at this posh museum of style can drop by to have their locks investigated for a consultation, and then wait on the model list until their services are needed.

THE CATCH A fee is charged, and you must wait on the model list for services.

Dipietro Todd

177 Post Street, Second Floor
(415) 693-5549 (model hotline)
http://dipietrotodd.com

Monday, 8:30 to 9:00 A.M. or 1:00 to 1:30 P.M.

Drop by this stylish, Downtown salon in person to show off your locks and consult with a student stylist during the hours above. Haircuts are $15; color starts at $20. Appointments will be scheduled on an individual basis, depending on the salon's need at the time. Unlike a school, you will be attended to by an experienced stylist, but all services are supervised by senior staff. You'll come out smelling like a rose for a song.

THE CATCH Haircuts are $15; color starts at $20.

Edo Salon

601 Haight Street
(415) 861-0131
www.edosalon.com

Models-to-be should drop by anytime and express their interest in a new future 'do. If the stylists are seeking your type, they will call you to set something up for one of their monthly demonstration cuts.

THE CATCH Haircuts cost $10 or less. Forget this as a resource for a reliable styling, but it could be a nice surprise if your needs coincide.

Elevations Salon and Café

451 Bush Street
(415) 392-2969
www.elevationsalon.com

Call to inquire about the current need for models for the on-site hair-cutting classes, but essentially, here's the drill: It takes two hours, and models must come by the salon/cafe for an initial consultation to show their hair length and type and to discuss what kind of new 'do they're looking for. This beautiful, upscale enter-

THE CATCH

Cuts are $15.

prise is huge, packed with art, and a bit of a scene unto itself. Modeling for Elevations is a good way to get a taste of it all for roughly the price of one of the organic salads and a latte from the house cafe.

Festoon Salon

1401 Martin Luther King Jr. Way, Berkeley
9 Claude Lane
(888) 357-2566
www.festoonsalon.com

To apply to be a hair model, fill out the Web site form every three months, after which time all applications are discarded. Students book a month in advance, so it can take

THE CATCH

A fee is charged. Haircuts take two to three hours; two to four hours for color. Gratuities are not included, and forty-eight hours' notice of a cancellation is required.

a while to get an appointment. But once you're in, you're gorgeous for a whole lot less: $15 to $25 for a haircut, and coloring starting at $20.

Gina Kahn Salon/Yosh for Hair

173 Maiden Lane
(415) 989-7704
www.ginakhan.com

In addition to a regular schedule of low-priced modeling opportunities for cut and color, there are also substantial special offers on their Web site that every style-

THE CATCH

Low-priced haircut and color opportunities; discounts for other beauty services.

conscious penny-pincher should be aware of, such as free hair treatments or complimentary nail service with the purchase of a regular cut and color. The offerings change frequently; check for what's on right now.

Goldstar Events Newsletter

www.goldstarevents.com

An excellent free subscription service for half-priced deals on massage and spa therapies from the city's top salons. See page 29 for more about this service's offerings.

International Academy of Precision Haircutting

638 Minna Street

(415) 934-9204

Sure, the $21 cut is hardly a giveaway. But the beauty of having your cut, color, or perm done here is that the person you're trusting to make you look good actually has the chops to do the job. Students are already licensed, practicing professionals just brushing up with a few classes to heighten and brighten their skills. The heads they work on will sparkle with that touch of professionalism that only experience can bring, and the styles will be what's hot on the hair horizon. Call for an appointment anytime classes are in session.

THE CATCH Haircuts are $21, but the students are professionals.

International College of Cosmetology

1224 Polk Street; (415) 931-6333, (415) 931-6363

3701 International Boulevard, Oakland; (510) 261-8256, (520) 261-3420

Drop-ins welcome Monday through Saturday, 8:30 A.M. to 5:00 P.M.

This large Vietnamese-American school of cosmetology has two locations, allowing them to double-down on the amount of skilled beauty practitioners who need bodies to practice on on both sides of the bay. You get discounted spa services: Prices start at just $4 for a shampoo, $7 for a cut, $4 for a manicure, and facials for $20. Waxing and more detailed services are also available.

THE CATCH A low fee is charged for work done by students. Plan to spend more time here than you would at your corner salon, but the financial savings are a good incentive.

Mara's Salon

112A Gough Street

(415) 552-5363 (hair and tanning)

(415) 368-7917 (nails and waxing)

www.marassalon.com

In addition to the 20 percent discount on all services (including hair, nails, waxing, and tanning) for first-time clients, this salon offers deals for the white and pasty: Two weeks of unlimited time on the tanning bed for just $45. If you refer a friend, you both get 20 percent off of any full-priced tanning package.

THE CATCH First-time customer discounts.

Miss Marty's Beauty School

1087 Mission Street

(415) 227-4240

www.missmartys.com

Professional and courteous, this full-service salon works just like any other, except that because your practitioner is gaining experience, you'll leave with your wallet lined a bit thicker than elsewhere. They offer a whole host of spa services, such as hair color that starts at $15, cuts from $8, manicures from $6, and even microdermabrasion sessions from just $80. Note that most services can be booked a day or two before, but if you're looking for a facial (starting at $35) it's best to book about a week in advance.

THE CATCH: Cuts start at $8, color at $15; manicures start at $6. Book facials in advance.

Moler Barber College

3815 Telegraph Avenue, Oakland

(510) 652-4177

Drop-ins Tuesday through Friday, 9:30 A.M. to 4:30 P.M.; Saturday, 10:30 A.M. to 4:30 P.M.

Like most barbershops, women may want to steer clear of this venue unless they just need a quick trim or desire a short, clean-cut 'do. Guys seeking the basics, however, have it made in the shade. In just ten or fifteen minutes, they can get the basic student haircut for $7. No appointments are necessary or given.

THE CATCH: The basic student cut is $7.

Mr. Pinkwhistle

580 Bush Street

(415) 989-7465

Informal and easygoing, this salon with the best name ever invites potential models to pop in anytime for a consultation with the stylist on staff and to make a future appointment for a new look. They seem to use a good amount of models on a regular basis, but their needs are always in flux.

THE CATCH: $20 cuts and $20 colors.

San Francisco Barber College

64 Sixth Street

(415) 621-6802

Wednesday, 8:30 A.M.

Men start lining up at 7:15 in the morning for the limited seating of these entirely free cuts. While there's no official policy that women can't/won't be chosen as models, don't expect to hold on to those lengthy tresses if you make it to the chair.

San Francisco Institute of Esthetics and Cosmetology

1067 Folsom, Suite 200
(415) 355-1734
www.sanfranciscoinstitute.com

Sure, that person wielding shears by your ears is in the learning stage, but all spa services are instructor supervised. The cost savings for you can be tremendous: $20 haircut and style, $40 for color, plus body scrubs, facials, waxing, etc.—some at about half the price of what you'd expect to pay elsewhere. Some services, such as manicures, cost about the same as they do elsewhere, but take twice as long, so be sure to leave extra room in your schedule for the learning curve.

THE CATCH

$20 haircut and style; $40 for color. Some services are not a bargain.

77 Maiden Lane Salon and Spa

77 Maiden Lane
(415) 391-7777
www.77maidenlane.com

Classes in cut and color are taught on alternating weeks at this lovely Union Square hot spot for your head. The best bet for hair models—a great bargain at $20 for cut or color, particularly for the color classes—is to get on the call list and wait it out. Don't expect a new 'do in time for a specific event. But if your schedule is flexible, this is a great way to go.

THE CATCH

$20 cuts and $20 colors for models on the call list.

Stephen Saiz Salon

560 Sutter Street
(415) 398-2345
stephensaizsalon.com

Tuesday

Call and check in often to learn about what hair type they're currently seeking. If the way you're growing it is what they're looking for, you will be invited to come in and sit as a model for their cutting class for the in-house stylists held one day a week. This is one of the few salons that is up front about the fact that there is no consultation with the models. The stylists will use you as they see fit, thus you have just a vague idea of what sort of style you may end up with before the scissors fly.

THE CATCH

The cut is free, but this is more of a "scalpal" donation than a service. The stylists will use your hair as they see fit.

Vidal Sassoon

359 Sutter Street

(415) 397-5105

Model drop-ins Thursday, 6:00 P.M.

The San Francisco location of this international learning mecca needs a whole host of models for various projects. Thus, they want you and your hair to drop by for a look-see on Thursday evenings (not more than thirty minutes or so) to meet with the stylists and to schedule you for the learning day that will suit you both the best. Expect the learning shampoo, cut, and style to take up to three hours—but hey, they don't look good unless you look good, right?

THE CATCH
Cuts are $16, color is $20. All services are cash only, gratuity not included.

Womack's Salon Academy

598 Silver Avenue

(415) 334-7774

Drop-ins Tuesday, 11:30 A.M. to 3:00 P.M.

Seniors and retirees are especially encouraged to drop by any Tuesday for a free cut and styling, but your locks can actually make you cash at this learning institution. Cheap Bastards will earn scores of cheapie points if they do the following: Sign up to help the Womack students pass their state board exams in Fairfield. Allow a student to cut your hair for free a couple of times. Then, ride with the student to Fairfield on the day of the exam to have your hair cut in front of an audience, and earn about a hundred bucks or so for your troubles. All arrangements are to be made between models and their student stylist; inquire within.

Zenzi's Cosmetology Training Center

551 Hayes Street

(415) 575-3540

www.zenzis.org

Tuesday to Saturday

Tony Hayes Valley is home to this equally posh learning institution in beauty education for almost seventy-five years. Excellent products, state-of-the-art facilities, and earnest students are the hallmark of the full range of spa services, which include everything from hair, nails, and waxing to facials and makeup application.

THE CATCH
Cuts start at $10, facials at $25, and color at $35.

MASSAGE AND BODYWORK

The Clinic at McKinnon Institute, LLC

2940 Webster Street
(510) 465-3488
www.mckinnonmassage.com

The school's professional massage services are available to the public at prices that won't rub you the wrong way: A complete toolbox of massage modalities are on hand for your relaxing pleasure, including acupressure, craniosacral, Swedish, reflexology, shiatsu, chair, pregnancy, deep tissue, and Thai massage. Call to schedule an appointment and speak with a practitioner.

THE CATCH One-hour massages start at $40.

Diamond Massage and Wellness Center

1841 Lombard Street
(415 921-1290
www.diamondwellness.com

Driven by a higher mission of community outreach and a quest for wellness and good health, these small practitioners offer financial incentives for various strata of the massage-needing public. A certain number of appointments are pro bono for qualifying recipients every month, and teachers receive a 10 percent discount at all times. Friends referring friends get a free massage. There are last-minute discounts, Web-only coupons for special services, and more. Log on to find out what's available this month.

THE CATCH Pro bono or discounted services given under certain circumstances

■ WORTH THE TRIP

ALIVE AND WELL INSTITUTE OF CONSCIOUS BODY WORK

150 Nellen Avenue, Corte Madera
(415) 945-9945
www.alivewell.com/html/massage.htm

North across the Golden Gate Bridge is a segue to pain-free living for those who suffer from chronic back issues. Progressive, innovative practices lie at the student hands of those practicing conscious bodywork and neuromuscular reprogramming, new ideas in physical and mental treatment for difficult discomfort. Massage treatments begin at $28 for fifty minutes. Learn more about the treatment and the services offered to the general public through the institution.

Stacy Simons, Certified Massage Therapist
(415) 254-4763
www.littleepiphany.com/massage.htm

Tuesday and Thursday, 11:00 A.M.

This private individual specializing in Swedish and deep-tissue massage reserves these two time slots every week for sliding-scale clients, first come, first served. Prices start at $35. The slots usually fill up quickly. She practices at a number of locations around SF, including the Mission, Downtown, and Ocean Boulevard. Read more about her background and the community services she offers at the link above.

THE CATCH

Two weekly time slots for sliding-scale services, with prices starting at $35. Slots fill quickly.

World School of Massage and Holistic Healing Arts

401 Thirty-second Avenue
(415) 221-2533
www.worldschoolmassage.com

Wednesday and Friday

You can be on the lucky receiving end of massage students in need of hands-on practice for a deep-tissue discount. Call the school to set up a late-afternoon appointment and inquire about which styles will be executed that week—shiatsu, Swedish, vibrational massage, or a panoply of others. Then let their fingers do the walking all over you on your way to relaxation.

THE CATCH

$40 for a one-hour massage.

{ FAMILY RESOURCES: }
OFF TO A CHEAP START

"The easiest way for your children
to learn about money is for you
not to have any."

—*Katharine Whitehorn*

All parents, particularly those of newborns and preschool-age children, need help wherever they can find it. In the case of the parent looking to make every penny sing, finding these family-boosting resources can be a great challenge. San Francisco may not be an ideal village for raising kids, but hey, we've got enough in the way of low-cost health care, free and low-cost child care, and stores selling half-price clothing and equipment to give it an honest go. Save your money for where it really counts: ice-cream cones, Vegas junkets for mom and dad, and your child's fixed-rate, local state school college tuition.

GENERAL PRENATAL, POSTNATAL, AND YOUNG CHILD RESOURCES

Bananas Childcare Referral and Support

5232 Claremont Avenue, Oakland
(510) 658-6046
www.bananasinc.org

With services offered in almost a dozen languages, this nonprofit agency helps connect parents with trained child care and offers a massive library, video collection, and collection of handouts on effective parenting. There's a free infant and child clothing exchange, and Bananas provides direction on subsidized child care for low-income caregivers.

Berkeley Parents Network

http://parents.berkeley.edu

This collective online repository and brain trust overflows with all of the Bay Area's resources for parents, babies, kids, and families and plenty of user experience and reviews to back it up. If you want it, there's also parenting advice galore, based on the knowledge of families associated with the University of California at Berkeley.

Family Ambassador Project
(415) 682-3239

This telephone hotline helps English- and Spanish-speaking parents track down a current list of parent education and support groups, many of which are free or low-cost. The hotline specializes in helping to uncover somewhat more obscure resources for all kinds of families, such as those speaking languages other than English or LGBT (lesbian, gay, bisexual, and transgender) families. Contact the project for the latest list of workshops about local resources and how to advocate for child services.

Family Paths
(510) 893-5444

Twenty-four hours a day, seven days a week, anyone from all over the Bay Area can phone this hotline for assistance with parental stress of any kind. Topics covered and references given tend to revolve around crisis intervention, counseling, and referrals to resources for children.

GoKid.org
www.gokid.org

Parents in the know subscribe to this free newsletter and online resource of fun activities and outings, safety and health information, social services, parenting resources, and other topics specific to the city of San Francisco. Though not quite as broad and as deep as the Berkeley Parents Network, GoKid is an indispensable tool for families in the West Bay.

Natural Resources
1367 Valencia Street
(415) 550-2611
www.naturalresources-sf.com

This prenatal and childbirth preparation center offers numerous resources for its paying clients, but it provides the following as a community service free to the public: Monthly "meet the doulas" and "meet the midwives" events connect new parents to practitioners, and a readily available library of binders help mom and dad find day care, babysitting, pediatricians, and alternative health professionals.

Nursing Mothers' Council
(415) 386-2229
www.nursingmothers.org

Free online pamphlets, telephone consultations, and home visits are offered to breastfeeding moms by volunteers, with no cost obligation to the public.

Parent's Place

1710 Scott Street
(415) 359-2454
www.jfcs.org

This comprehensive family support service organization through Jewish Family and Children's Services offers sliding-scale workshops, play groups, development groups, mentoring, resources for dads, and more.

Postpartum Depression Hotline

(888) 773-7090

Daily, 9:00 A.M. to 9:00 P.M.

Callers leave their first name and a phone number, and a volunteer who has survived PPD will return the call same day. In addition to providing someone to talk to, the volunteers will refer new moms to self-help resources and a handful of low-cost professionals. The call and the service are free.

San Francisco General Women's Health Center

1001 Potrero Avenue
(415) 206- 3409

This public hospital owned by the city offers its services to all residents, with free or low-cost services based on individual eligibility. No one is turned away, and services are offered in English, Spanish, and Chinese.

THE CATCH
In our experience, lines are long, and those seeking information can expect lengthy delays.

Telephone Aid in Living with Kids (TALK)

1757 Waller Street
(415) 387-3864
www.talklineforparents.org

This organization offers a host of community services for parents at the risk of burnout, including workshops, drop-in sessions on parenting skills, substance abuse assistance, counseling, group support, and child play groups. The signature community benefit is the twenty-four-hour crisis and counseling telephone line for parents to call for support, information, and referrals.

THE CATCH
Services are free, but some require preregistration.

SAFETY FIRST

San Francisco Department of Public Health's Children's Environmental Health Promotion
1390 Market Street, Suite 230
(415) 554-8930 (lead poisoning prevention)
(415) 554-8930, ext. 11 (asthma information)
www.sfgov.org/site/frame.asp?u=www.dph.sf.ca.us/

In an effort to raise healthy children in a city full of century-old homes, this public service says it will come to your house and help educate your family on the risks of lead poisoning in children, coordinate medical intervention in lead poisoning cases, identify lead hazards, and advise property owners (you or your landlord) on safe remediation methods. Families of asthma sufferers can also receive information on the physicality and treatment of the disease, assistance implementing environmental controls, home assessment, some free home control devices (like new air filters), and referrals to other social services.

San Francisco Police Department Child Safety Program, *(415) 575-6363. Call this number and arrange a visit with a police officer to ensure that your infant car seat has been properly installed.*

San Francisco Water Department, *(877) 737-8297. This public utility can be difficult to navigate, but it will do free lead testing of your home water supply.*

Women and Children's Health Referral Line at the Department of Public Health
(800) 300-9950

This local service agency points parents toward health-care options for their children, particularly for parents who are seeking advice in disability prevention and for youngsters with special needs. While the agency's services—such as WIC, AIM, Healthy Kids, and MediCal—are of most interest to low-income families, the agency can point anyone toward low-cost clinics, classes, and other services.

Universal Home Visiting Program of the Department of Public Health
30 Van Ness Avenue
(415) 575-5727, (415) 575-5705

Regardless of income, language, or hospital affiliation, the city will send a public health nurse to your home for a free newborn and new mother exam within a week after delivery. Patients are usually referred to this program through their birthing hospital, but any citizen is welcome to call and arrange a visit postpartum.

PARENT/BABY/KID PLAY GROUPS AND SOCIALIZING

City College of San Francisco Department of Child Development and Family Studies Parent and Infant and Parent and Child Classes
(415) 561-1921
www.ccsf.edu/Departments/Child_Development/programs.html

When the college has courses in session, it encourages parents and children—newborns to kindergarteners—to attend no-cost play groups in the child development program. Certified instructors head up these gatherings, child development students learn from the study participants, and the kids get a great play session with others their own age. Parents are often interviewed about their child and their role and may receive tips on health, safety, and daily routines. Download this semester's schedule of class times and locations.

Congregation Sha'ar Zahav
290 Dolores Street
(415) 861-6932
www.shaarzahav.org

In addition to a for-pay religious school and programs for teens, this LGBT temple in the Mission offers monthly baby meeting groups and tot Shabbat programs that invite the public to come and meet the congregation at no cost.

Congregation Sherith Israel

2266 California Street
(415) 346-1720
www.sherithisrael.org

Check the calendar for a whole month filled with meet-and-greets for babies, kids, and families. Weekly meetings of preschool kids of all ages are slated alongside moms' groups, dads' groups, baby-friendly yoga classes, music classes, tot Shabbat, and heaps more. Families of all faiths are welcome. Many gatherings are free, offer a free first visit, or are otherwise affordable to the community at large.

Golden Gate Mothers Group

www.ggmg.org

Yes, it does cost money to be a part of this club, but moms of young children get an awful lot for their dollar. In addition to the group newsletter and e-mail discus-

THE CATCH

Membership is $55 a year. Nannies and spouses are not welcome to many of the activities.

sion list, there are regular monthly educational meetings, organized play groups, holiday events, welcome teas, and the like.

NoeStrolls

Meets at Holey Bagel, 3872 24th Street
www.noestrolls.com

Thursday, 11:00 A.M.

Their motto: Keep those babies rolling. The stroller-pushing Noe Valley-focused baby brigade meets in droves in front of the bagel shop where, thanks to their parental status, they are awarded a free baby bagel. Then they head down the Castro hill and turn onto 18th Street, at which point they stop to schmooze amid the playground of Dolores Park. This group is active, with an excellent Web site of resources and daily kid activities, plus some career enrichment programs and events on the roster.

Peakaboutique's Tot Parties

1306 Castro Street
(415) 641-6192

Last Thursday of the month, 6:00 P.M.

This popular used children's goods store in Noe Valley invites its shoppers and its neighbors in for free wine for mom and dad, free juice for the kids, and an opportunity to foster a little bit of community around the pursuit of retail.

TIP

During the summer months this event may be canceled due to travel schedules. It's a good idea to call and confirm before attending.

The Seven Principles Project

(415) 581-2458

www.sevenprinciples.org

Community awareness, community action, and community development are part of the impetus for this group dedicated to the care and growth of SF's African-American newborns as established by the Department of Public Health. Bayview/Hunters Point area events include nights of free movies and dinner as a way to foster community and parents meeting with other parents.

AFTER-SCHOOL PROGRAMS AND CHILD CARE

Babysitter Exchange

www.babysitterexchange.com

Though not specific just to parents in the Bay Area, this online co-op allows parents situated near one another to meet, gain trust, and watch one another's kids—all without costing anyone a dime. You contribute time and evenings in, but you get the same in return, if you can find like-minded members of your community to share in your pursuit to get out of the house. It's a bit cumbersome to get an exchange started, but once it's up and running, this is the best thing since dinner and a movie.

Boys and Girls Clubs of San Francisco

88 Kearny Street, Twelfth Floor

(415) 445-5437

www.bgcsf.org

After-school programs at each location vary. Contact the center nearest you to inquire about availability and rates.

Children's Council of San Francisco

445 Church Street
(415) 343-3300
www.childrenscouncil.org

Second Tuesday of the month, 6:00 to 8:00 P.M.

This is an opportunity to meet other parents in need of child care for a potential swapping of services, organized nanny share, or co-op. Parents from all over are welcome to attend free information workshops to learn about child-care options as well as about the legal obligations of care providers, licensing regulations for day-care operations, screening tests for potential care providers, and more. Care for children older than babies-in-arms can be arranged at least one week in advance.

THE CATCH

 Registration is required.

Downtown Berkeley YMCA Childwatch Program, KidZone, and Kids' Night Out

2001 Allston Way, Berkeley
(510) 848-9622
www.baymca.org

Similar to YMCA programs offered elsewhere, here the two-hour-max Childwatch program welcomes children as young as eight weeks and as old as seven years. KidZone is free with membership ($40 adults/$25 kids) for children ages six to thirteen. Kids' Night Out is a scheduled, summer camp environment offered about once a month, always on a Saturday night, where kids swim, play games, and do arts and crafts for a flat child-care fee that's a lot less than what you'd pay a babysitter. Advanced registration is required.

THE CATCH

An extra dollar fee is added per diaper change, and parents are fined $5 for every ten minutes they go over the two-hour limit

Note that other East Bay YMCAs offer additional child-care and play activities for children of all ages at significantly reduced fees.

Kidspace at the LBGT Center

1800 Market Street
(415) 865-5553
www.sfcenter.org/kidspace.php
ariannec@sfcenter.org (reservations)

Tuesday, Thursday, and Friday, 5:30 P.M. to 8: 30 P.M.; Saturday, 9:30 A.M. to 5:30 P.M.

Whether dad and dad or mom and mom (or sometimes, even mom and dad) are popping in for a meeting or support group, attending a social function, or just stopping in to use their laptop at Three Dollar Bill Cafe, parents will kick up their rainbow high heels to learn that free and donation-based child care and supervised group play is available by prearranged reservation for tots from infant to school age. Junior is cared for by skilled and certified educators and interacts with other kids of LGBT parents for arts and crafts, story time, dancing, etc.

THE CATCH
Registration required.

USED PREGNANCY, BABY, AND KID SUPPLY STORES

Why pay top dollar for new clothes and toys they'll outgrow in a New York minute? Buy it used—or sell it when you're done—at any of these local retailers:

Bug, *648 Chenery Street; (415) 239-9534.*

Chloe's Closet, *451A Cortland Avenue; (415) 642-3300; www.chloes closet.com.*

MaternityXchange.com. *Locations vary; get on the mailing list to learn about their regular designer maternity clothing sales around the Bay Area.*

Miranda's Mama, *4000 Balboa Street; (415) 831-2988; www.mirandas mama.com.*

Peakaboutique, *1306 Castro Street; (415) 641-6192.*

Town School Clothes Closet, *3325 Sacramento Street; (415) 929-8019.*

And of course, what would any kind of shopping be without Craigslist.org and eBay.com. . . .

Richmond YMCA Childwatch Program

360 Eighteenth Avenue
(415) 666-9622
www.ymcasf.org/Richmond

Monday through Friday, 8:30 A.M. to 12:30 P.M.; Saturday, 8:45 A.M. to 1:00 P.M.

In addition to low-cost before- and after-school child care, the Richmond Y offers supervised care for your child, ages six months to twelve years, for a maximum of two hours while you take a class and work out; the fee is $4 an hour. Adults must remain on premises, but with a full calendar of dance, yoga, cardio classes, and muscle conditioning, there will be plenty to do to give your body a workout and your parenting mind a break.

Note that many other YMCA branches offer inexpensive before-school, after-school, and summer camp programs as well. For more information visit www.ymcasf.org.

San Francisco Beacon Initiative

1390 Market Street, Suite 900
(415) 554-8967
www.sfbeacon.org

A number of after-school programs and homework help opportunities are found at nine locations around the city.

San Francisco Recreation and Parks' Latchkey Program

(415) 715-4065
http://parks.sfgov.org

All children who are San Francisco residents between the ages of six and twelve qualify for this city-run after-school and summer camp program at deeply discounted rates. For child care from 2:00 to 6:00 P.M. during the school year, parents pay just $94.50—half that if they qualify for financial assistance. Full-day summer care programs are also offered for a fraction of what one would expect to pay at a private day-care center. The program happens at sixteen different locations around SF; consult the Web site to find the location that's most convenient for your family as well as current registration information.

Wu Yee Children's Services

706 Mission Street, Sixth Floor
(415) 677-0100, (415) 391-4956 (referral line)
www.wuyee.org

This is a great place for parents to learn about their child-care options. Staff members provide workshops on identifying quality child care, and they can help families determine if their income level qualifies them for defrayed child-care costs or for city or government programs. Many other child services are offered in a number of languages to help families on the grow.

{ KID STUFF: } BIG FUN FOR SMALL CHANGE

"Industry, thrift, and self-control
are not sought because they
create wealth, but because they
create character."

–Calvin Coolidge

Making children is fun and free. Why does entertaining them have to cost so much? It doesn't, if you're a savvy parent who knows where to find a bargain in children's entertainment. For toddler or teenager, there are about a zillion ways to amuse the whippersnappers around the Bay. And while this is by no means a complete list, here are a few of the most interesting and innovative. Pack up a stack of PB&Js and you needn't even give in to the cries of "lunch!" This is homespun fun at its best.

Breakfast with Enzo

LMNO Music with Enzo Garcia
Bernal Heights Neighborhood Center
515 Cortland Street
(415) 652-2474
www.enzogarcia.com

Saturday, 10:00 A.M. to noon

It's strictly BYO at this free weekend morning affair—bring your own breakfast. While you munch you will be entertained with song, rhythm, movement, and melody for infants, children, and preschoolers by this niche musician of the accordion, banjo, and song. If you like what you see during this weekend performance, you can sign up for the artist's pay session weekly meetings in small, interactive groups.

THE BIG DIP
FOR SMALL FRIES

Swimming lessons for kids are provided at the following city pools during the summer season. Costs vary a bit, but most charge just $1 for children and $4 for adults.

Balboa Pool, *San Jose Avenue and Havelock; (415) 337-4701*

Coffman Pool, *Visitacion and Hahn; (415) 337-4702*

Garfield Pool, *26th Street and Harrison; (415) 695-5001*

Martin Luther King Jr. Pool, *3rd Street and Carroll; (415) 822-2807*

North Beach Pool, *Lombard and Mason; (415) 391-0435*

Rossi Pool, *Arguello Boulevard and Anza; (415) 666-7014*

Carousel in Golden Gate Park
Martin Luther King Jr. Drive and Bowling Green Drive
(415) 812-2725

Adjacent to the newly renovated Golden Gate Park Children's Playground (now called Koret Children's Quarter), this classic carved merry-go-round is a must-see tourist attraction packed with charm and nostalgia—oh, and the kids will like it, too. Calliope music, sprightly horses that bob up and down, and the much-coveted teacup seat make this a ride to remember and a great part of spending a lovely day in the park. And for the price, riding the carousel is worth it for the photo ops alone.

THE CATCH }
$1.50 for adults, $.50 for kids ages six to twelve.

Cartoon Art Museum

655 Mission Street
(415) CAR-TOON
www.cartoonart.org

One Saturday a month, 1:00 to 3:00 P.M.

Kids ages eight to fourteen are encouraged to come learn about this exciting, kid-friendly medium one panel at a time. Topics covered include character design, storyboarding, and the creation of their own mini comic book. The calendar changes often, so call to inquire about upcoming classes. Classes and materials are free with the price of museum admission. Weeklong summer camps are also offered for roughly $100 for five days of instruction.

THE CATCH — Admission is $5.

Children's Fairyland

699 Bellevue Avenue, Oakland
(510) 452-2259
www.fairyland.org

For the preschool set, this magical miniland—where classic children's stories come to life alongside farm animals, storybooks, and puppet shows—is the kiddie amusement park that can kick a certain giant mouse's tail any day. Parents lounge in the shade while young explorers take on rides and plenty of safe bridges, waterways, and play structures. Best of all, it's a stunning view across Lake Merritt and an easy walk from BART. It ain't free, but your six bucks buys unlimited rides, making the value giant sized.

THE CATCH — Admission is $6.

Circus Center

755 Frederick Street
(415) 759-8123
www.circuscenter.org

Sunday, 6:00 and 7:00 P.M.

Crack that whip. Juggle that ball. Ladies, gentlemen, and children of all ages are welcome not just to watch the circus arts at this full-time school offering myriad classes, but also to participate and learn a few tricks. On Sunday evening real circus knowledge can be yours for the price of a bag of peanuts. At 6:00 P.M. anyone is welcome to get their whip-cracking skills cracking, and at 7:00 your four bucks buys three hours of juggling instruction. Drop-ins are welcome. You may not fly through the air with the greatest of ease, but hey, it's better than being shot out of a cannon. . . .

THE CATCH — Each class is $4 ($8 for both).

Fortune Cookie Factory

261 12th Street, Oakland
(510) 832-5552

Yes, Virginia, there are other fortune cookie factories to visit in SF's Chinatown, but this is the *real* deal both in size and scope, it's one of the oldest, and it's the only one that can truly accommodate large groups. It's worth crossing the bridge to Oakland and paying the buck admission to have an opportunity to put your own message inside a cookie; an order of 1,000 is just $12. Your admission fee includes a small bag of cookies.

THE CATCH

Admission is $1;
a reservation is required
for groups of ten or more.

SAN FRANCISCO REC CENTERS THAT OFFER FREE COOKING CLASSES TO KIDS

Douglass Playground, 26th Street and Douglass; (415) 695-5017

Eugene Friend Rec Center, 270 6th Street; (415) 554-9532

Hayes Valley Playground, Hayes and Buchanan; (415) 554-9526

Herz Playground, Visitacion and Hahn; (415) 337-4706

Joseph Lee Recreation Center, 1395 Mendell; (415) 822-9040

Midtown Terrace Playground, Clarendon and Olympia Way; (415) 753-7036

Minnie and Lovie Ward Rec Center, Capitol and Montana; (415) 337-4710

Miraloma Playground, Omar and Sequoia Way; (415) 337-4704

Parque Ninos Unidos, 23rd Street and Treat; (415) 282-7461

Tenderloin Recreation Center, 570 Ellis; (415) 753-2761

Upper Noe Recreation Center, Day and Sanchez; (415) 695-5011

Youngblood Coleman Playground, Mendell and Galvez; (415) 695-5005

MOCHA Museum of Children's Art

538 Ninth Street, Oakland
(510) 465-8770
www.mocha.org

Tuesday through Friday, 10:00 A.M. to 5:00 P.M.

Get your eighteen-month-old (or older) interested in art and expression at this massive workshop space ready to accept paint-splattered creativity on a drop-in basis. Go with the museum's weekly theme or simply let your youngsters' imagination run wild—either way, for the cost of a box of crayons, they can unleash their little artist inside. While you're there, plant the seeds of art appreciation in the adorable, child-powered, and surprisingly potent exhibit hall.

THE CATCH: $5 drop-in fee for hands-on creativity, but entrance to the gallery is free.

Musee Mecanique

Pier 45, Shed A (at the end of Taylor Street)
(415) 346-2000
www.museemechanique.org

Laughing Sal, an eight-foot mechanical puppet behind glass from the turn of the twentieth century, is downright creepy as she cackles away. But this entirely unique arcade of automated flip books, hand-powered robots, and entire carnivals made from lit-up toothpicks is completely fascinating and a wonderful historical window into how people got their jollies along the waterfront before the advent of electronic video games (though a few of those are on hand, too). This is absolutely a must-see, not just for kids but even for adults. It's worth braving the tourism and traffic of Fisherman's Wharf—yes, it's that good. Best of all, it costs nothing to walk in the door and pocket change to make the magic happen. And if you time it right, you can enjoy the player pianos on someone else's quarter.

THE CATCH: Most amusements cost 25 cents.

Randall Museum

199 Museum Way
(415) 554-9600
www.randallmuseum.org

In addition to being an extremely cool museum geared toward younger kids with a great playground and lots of hands-on activities, Randall Museum offers regular and drop-in arts and craft classes in clay, woodworking, magic lessons, and heaps more by the barrel. Admission to the museum is free; most classes are $4. Kids are also welcome to feed the critters in the small animal petting zoo or operate the impressive model train city, both activities on Saturday only.

THE CATCH: Most classes are $4.

A MOVIE NIGHT GUARANTEED
TO MAKE SOMEONE CRY

Parkway Theater Baby Brigade
1834 Park Boulevard, Lake Merritt, Oakland
(510) 814-2400
www.picturepubpizza.com
Monday, 6:30 P.M. and 7:00 P.M.

Don't bother turning off your cell phone. You may not get to see the entire film, but at $5 per adult, chances are you're paying half of what you normally would anyway. Dinner and a movie is still an option for you and your baby under one year. The pizza, beer, and comfy couch environment of this theater makes it a lot cozier than other screening houses, and no one will "shush" you because they'll be too busy shushing their own.

Redwood Valley Railway
Tilden Regional Park, Berkeley
Grizzly Peak and Lomas Cantadas
(510) 548-6100
www.redwoodvalleyrailway.com

This massive green space in the East Bay offers swimming at Lake Anza, the wonder of the petting zoo, the enjoyment of the carousel, and the opportunity to just roll around in the splendor. But it's the child-sized steam train that young kids and train enthusiasts return to again and again for twelve minutes of steam-powered bliss. All aboard! And note that your dog can ride for free.

THE CATCH
Tickets are $2, or five for $8.

San Francisco Maritime National Historical Park

National Park Service

Hyde Street Pier (Hyde and Beach Streets)

(415) 447-5000

www.nps.gov/safr/local/calendar.html

While there are some hefty fees for touring the fleet of ancient shipping vessels and the submarine, the USS *Pampanito,* the Maritime offers up a tremendous amount of free, nautically themed events of interest to older kids with a lust for the pirate's life and an interest in SF's history as a port city. Particularly in summer, programs like sea chantey sing-alongs, a tour of the collection's small crafts via boat ride to Alameda, bird-watching tours, crafts, and ships' radio demonstrations abound. Check the calendar and ahoy, ahoy.

WORTH THE TRIP

JELLY BELLY FACTORY TOUR

1 Jelly Belly Lane, Fairfield

(800) 9-JELLYBEAN

www.jellybelly.com

One hour's drive north of San Francisco, the colorful, sweet magic happens. This mammoth jelly bean factory will not only entertain you during the totally free forty-minute walking tour, but not a single parent or child walks out without a generous bag of free candy. Pair that with all the samples given in the storefront following the tour and voilà!—high-fructose lunch. On display are excellent mosaics of Ronald Reagan, Elvis Presley, Marilyn Monroe, and other celebrity classic figures forever commemorated in the Day-Glo candy. The huge factory of brilliantly hued working turbines is truly a sight to behold.

> **TIP** Midweek tours, when the factory workers are actually on-site, are much, much better than the weekend video-only tours.

YOUNG EAGLES AT THE HILLER AVIATION MUSEUM

San Carlos Airport
620 Airport Drive, San Carlos
(650) 654-0200
www.hiller.org/young-eagles.shtml

Third Saturday of the month, 11:00 A.M. to 1:00 P.M.

In an effort to boost interest in the fancy and freedom of flight, the non-profit EAA Aviation Foundation offers children ages eight to seventeen a free flight in a small plane piloted by a credited pilot over the clouds of the Bay Area. Your kids are welcome to earn their wings on a first come, first served basis—but get there early, as this tends to be insanely crowded, particularly in summer.

San Francisco Public Library

(415) 557-4400

www.sfpl.org (click on "events")

The events and locations change every month, but one thing is always constant: the tremendous amount of no-cost activities offered for kids from birth through their teens. From story times, sing-alongs, and baby bounces to puppet shows and Banned Books Reading Clubs for older kids, there is truly something at every city branch to stimulate the mind of children of all ages. These are your tax dollars at work, people, so be sure to crack the cover and take advantage.

Scharffen Berger Factory Tour

914 Heinz, Berkeley

(510) 981-4066

www.scharffenberger.com

The thing that makes this free tour so delicious is, well, that it's a tour of a chocolate factory! And the Wonka-esque antique machinery imported from Europe is a feast for the eyes as much as the aromas are a feast for the senses. Even the most

THE CATCH Reservations are a necessity. Samples are offered, but not as many as we would like.

die-hard chocoholic will learn something about how the dark god is crafted, and I challenge you to try to avoid buying a hot chocolate from the cafe by tour's end.

Shan-Yee Poon Ballet School

www.poonballet.com

Ever wonder what your toddler would look like in a tutu? How about your teenager in tap shoes? Parents are welcome to this serious dance school's frequent orienta-

THE CATCH Free first class.

tion programs, and their children are welcome to test out a class for free before committing to a hefty prepaid schedule. In addition to ballet, the school offers jazz, tap, and more to the lithe and graceful. Be careful. Your kid may just love it.

Studio 39's Magic Carpet Ride

Pier 39, the Embarcadero

(415) 397-3939

In an entirely over-touristed part of town, it's rare to find any kind of free entertainment. But when you've grown tired of listening to the seals and taking in the silver-painted street performers, this is a chance for you and yours to be the star of the show. Step in front of the blue screen, ham it up, and "fly" above the sights

THE CATCH Making the video is free; there's a steep fee to purchase a copy.

of SF in your own five-minute video. If you like what you see you'll have to shell out forty bucks to take home a copy. Don't blame us if you get suckered in. We're just letting you know that the making of the video is free.

SAN FRANCISCO REC CENTERS THAT OFFER FREE ARTS AND CRAFTS FOR KIDS

Let your school-age Picassos unleash their right brain at the following locations. Students needn't bring anything but their imagination. Schedules change often; it's a good idea to call and confirm.

Bernal Heights Playground, *500 Moultrie; (415) 695-5007*

Boedekker Park, *240 Eddy; (415) 292-2019*

Christopher Playground, *5210 Diamond Heights Boulevard; (415) 695-5000*

Douglass Playground, *26th Street and Douglass; (415) 695-5017*

Gilman Playground, *Gillman Avenue and Bill Walsh Way; (415) 467-4566*

Grattan Playground, *1180 Stanyan; (415) 753-7039*

Hamilton Recreation Center, *1900 Geary Boulevard; (415) 292-2008*

Hayes Valley Playground, *Hayes and Buchanan; (415) 554-9526*

Hellen Wills Playground, *Broadway and Larkin; (415) 359-1281*

Joe DiMaggio Playground, *651 Lombard; (415) 391-0437*

Julius Kahn Playground; *West Pacific Avenue and Spruce; (415) 292-2004*

Eugene Friend Rec Center, *270 6th Street; (415) 554-9532*

Tenderloin Recreation Center, *570 Ellis; (415) 753-2761*

Youngblood Coleman Playground, *Mendell and Galvez; (415) 695-5005*

Tiny Tots, a project of San Francisco Recreation and Parks
(415) 666-7079

http://parks.sfgov.org

Since the 1950s kids ages nine months to five years have been gathering at rec centers, pools, and parks all over the city in organized droves of play for about half the cost of privately organized play groups. Instructors rely on parent attendance and support, and in turn they try to provide kids with an array of age-appropriate learning and fun activities that build self-esteem and social skills. Download this season's PDF from the Web site and find a session that's right for your child and your schedule.

THE CATCH } $4 a session, or ten sessions for $30.

Yerba Buena Gardens Festival
760 Howard Street

(415) 543-1718

www.ybgf.org

May to October

Loads of free kid events and kid-friendly cultural happenings are a part of this summerlong extravaganza. For more info, see page 46.

{ SHOPPING:
BARGAINS FOR THE
CHIC CHEAP ELITE }

"The excellence of a gift lies
in its appropriateness
rather than in its value."

–Charles Dudley Warner

Why pay more when you don't have to? San Francisco is your grandmother's dream closet of all kinds of vintage, old-school, and used stuff just ripe for the plucking—so much so that the choices can be overwhelming. But as the world of commerce surrounding vintage and shabby chic can attest, just because an item is old or previously owned does not mean that it will cost any less than if you bought its brand-new counterpart. In fact, Haight Street, Union Street, and the Mission especially can be guilty of charging deeply bloated prices for eighties miniskirts and Scooby-Doo lunch boxes simply because there is a captive audience to pay it. Enough is enough! "Antiques" and "collectibles" need not apply. This is not a directory of all the secondhand and consignment shops in town—it's simply a list of the best of those with their heads on straight when it comes to knowing what low-priced goods should actually cost.

TOTALLY FREE STUFF

Craigslist's "Free" and "Barter" Categories
www.craigslist.org

My Honda Civic for your pick-up truck, my massage therapy for your Spanish lessons, my encyclopedias or dirt pile or moving boxes or queen-sized futon totally free if you come and get it. . . . The possibilities are endless and manifold, but it all comes down to the same basic idea—getting stuff or trading stuff with members of your local community, no cash involved. If you're seeking something specific, this can be a great way to find it. Or if you have that compulsive shopping gene and you're short on cash, it's a great way to "catalog shop" without costing a dime. These lists are popular and change frequently, so keep your eyes peeled, act fast, and ye shall be rewarded.

Kiehl's

2360 Fillmore Street; (415) 359-9260

Inside Neiman Marcus, 150 Stockton Street; (415) 362-3900

Inside Saks Fifth Avenue, 384 Post Street; (415) 986-4300

www.kiehls.com

Sure, the stores are located in ritzy shopping districts, but that just makes this free-loader's delight that much more pleasurable. Come in looking well scrubbed and they'll be happy to part with a free sample of any of their high-end body care and hygiene products. And with purchase, they'll practically give away the whole shop for free—a great way to try and not have to buy.

San Francisco Chronicle's Free Stuff Classified Ads

www.sfgate.com

Check the paper. Most of the free stuff is crap, but people have been known to dispose of their upright pianos this way.

San Francisco Freecycle Network

www.freecycle.org

Join this local chapter of the international phenomenon and let your in-box receive the bulk and bounty that the Bay Area has to offer. People pony up all kinds of one-man's-trash-another-man's-treasure goods and services that are ripe for the picking, free of charge, and simply available to any who come forward to claim them. Of course, you can also get rid of unwanted items in this forum as well. If you've got a whole apartment or clubhouse to furnish, or you're seeking a way to outfit your Burning Man camp on the super-duper cheap, this is an invaluable resource.

San Francisco Really Really Free Market

Dolores Park (18th and Dolores Streets)
www.sf-rrfm.org

Last Saturday of the month, noon to 4:00 P.M.

It's all free. Every damn thing, and that selection varies based on who showed up and what they brought. Essentially, this is the equivalent of finding someone's discarded goods in the street, but it's conveniently located all in one place, next to a whole bunch of other stuff that no one else wants. You can get lucky, and you're likely to score if you're looking for clothes, books, bread, or what have you. This event also packs a political punch, with an anticapitalist slant in favor of the "gift economy." Feel free to donate what's been cluttering your closets.

WHY BUY WHEN YOU CAN BORROW?

The cash conscious are well aware of the public library as a resource for books, DVDs, CDs, and other media, but there are additional libraries on the shelf that will let you check out other goods as well.

Children's Council Toy Lending Library, *445 Church Street; (415) 276-2900; www.childrenscouncil.org. Free and low-cost playthings can be borrowed for up to a month at a time. This is a great way to minimize clutter in the toy box.*

San Francisco Tool Lending Center, *1016 Howard Street; (415) 552-9201; www.sfcleancity.com/tool-lending/index.html. An operation of the Clean City Coalition, this excellent resource is scheduled to reopen sometime in late 2007.*

Temescal Tool Lending Library, *5205 Telegraph Avenue, Oakland; (510) 597-5089; www.oaklandlibrary.org/Branches/temtll.htm. More than 2,700 do-it-yourself aids are stashed here, along with a great selection of instructional videos and DVDs. Occasional free workshops round out the mix.*

Stop AIDS Project
207 Sanchez Street
(415) 575-0747
www.stopaids.org

Oh, come on. You've been called a cheap f**ker before. If, in your case, this is actually true (and you know it is), stop by here anytime to stock up on condoms and personal lubricant gratis. You can use all the cash you've saved to buy your potential boy/girlfriend a drink (during happy hour only, of course).

99 CENTS STORES

What can a dollar buy these days? Not much . . . except at these locations.

Divisadero 99 Cents Plus Store, *777 Divisadero Street; (415) 567-9117*

Golden 99 Cents Zone, *5 Leland Avenue; (415) 333-3923*

99 Cents & Over Discount Outlet, *2205 Mission Street; (415) 647-9495*

99 Cents Only Stores, *2558 Mission Street; (415) 647-5382*

Sunset Scavenger's Waste Access Control Program/Household Hazardous Waste
501 Tunnel Avenue
(415) 330-1405

Home Depot it isn't, but if you come and pick them up, there are multiple five-gallon tubs of free latex paint—and only paint—available for the taking. Recipients have their choice of three charming colors—off-white and the more obscure off-red and off-green—house-made composites of all paint donations received, mixed together in the hopes of giving it to someone who can use it.

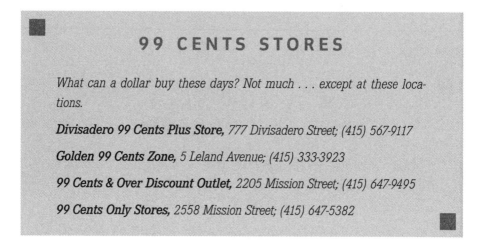

REAL THRIFT STORES (THE KIND THAT BENEFIT CHARITY)

Community Thrift Store
623 Valencia Street
(415) 861-4910

This is an awesome place for shopping and donating; those dropping off a carload have their choice of dozens of different charities for their belongings to benefit. There's an excellent selection of Christmas holiday goods available year-round (should you need them) plus a frequently refreshed pile of good, stylish vintage clothes; cheap books; records; and great furniture. It's all at excellent prices, particularly for the neighborhood.

THE CATCH
Service can be a little slack, but at these prices, who cares? }

Goodwill Industries

1580 Mission Street (flagship store); (415) 575-2240

820 Clement Street; (415) 668-3635

86 11th Street; (415) 575-2197

1700 Fillmore Street; (415) 441-2159

822 Geary Street; (415) 922-0405

1700 Haight Street; (415) 387-1192

2279 Mission Street; (415) 826-5759

4631 Mission Street; (415) 239-8070

3801 3rd Street, Suite 330; (415) 641-4470

61 West Portal Avenue; (415) 665-7291

www.sfgoodwill.org

The local locations of the nationwide chain are a great place to pick up work clothes for that temp job in corporate America or whenever you need cast-off department store "normal" clothes at bottom-barrel prices. Knickknacks can be hit or miss.

Junior League Next-to-New Shop

2226 Fillmore Street

(415) 567-1627

If you've come to the neighborhood to shop at Seconds to Go, this spot, a couple of doors down, is also worth a stop.

Oakland Museum White Elephant Sale

333 Lancaster Street, Oakland

(510) 536-6800

www.museumca.org/events/elephant.html

This monstrous, annual springtime fund-raiser for the Oakland Museum has been happening for almost fifty years for good reason: It is a mind-blowing, department-store selection of everything in a warehouse almost 100,000 square feet. While prices aren't as cheap as they could be (hey, this is a fund-raiser, after all), they're still pretty good, particularly if you're patient and willing to sort through a whole lot of trash to find that treasure. Clothes, furniture, sporting equipment, collectibles, books, music, and so very much more make it worthy of marking your calendar up to a year in advance. Check the Web site to see when the next event will be.

Out of the Closet Thrift Store

100 Church Street; (415) 252-1101

1295 Folsom Street; (415) 558-7176

1498 Polk Street; (415) 771-1503

This relative newcomer to the royalty of the local thrifting court is a great overall spot for used clothes and kitchen goods. This project of the AIDS Healthcare Foundation donates its proceeds to finding a cure; as a result they have a somewhat better selection of used men's clothes than your average Goodwill.

Salvation Army Thrift Store

1185 Sutter Street; (415) 771-3818

1501 Valencia Street; (415) 401-0337

Shop carefully at these locations; particularly on Valencia, where items can sometimes be overpriced and still covered in stains. Prices in the "better goods" section of the store near the front can sometimes be negotiated with manager approval, but not always same day. Still, this is a giant thrifting opportunity, and bargains abound for the shrewd eyed and intrepid.

WORTH THE TRIP

WORTH THE TRIP

SALVATION ARMY PROCESSING FACILITY AND REHAB CENTER

200 Lytton Springs Road, Healdsburg
(707) 433-3334

About an hour and a half north of San Francisco, this massive, outlying sorting facility is a Disneyland of household goods. You need a new fan? Check out the massive tables filled with hundreds of models. Looking for a new coffeepot or waffle iron? You'll have an entire room to choose from. Toys, household goods, etc., are widely available and ready to move—the only thing that's a little thin is the clothing room, which is just average, but can still unleash some pretty good finds. A snack bar is on premises to fuel your shopping pleasure.

Seconds to Go

2252 Fillmore Street
(415) 563-7806

While not exactly drop-dead cheap, this well-stocked clothes closet on the posh part of Fillmore carries an impressive selection of designer clothes—among them Anne Klein and Prada for men and women—at a fraction of what you'd pay for the same new. Still, it might be $40 garments rather than $400, but a bargain is in the eye of the beholder.

Segunda Vuelta

1328 Valencia Street
(415) 285-9652

Monday through Wednesday, 10:00 A.M. to 3:00 P.M.

This tiny, eclectic secondhand shop benefits the glassy, supermodern Bethel Christian Church across the street. Despite SF's insane real estate and rental prices, here prices are kept Midwest state low: clothes for $3, knickknacks for as little as a quarter. All of this, of course, is a magnified bargain when compared to Valencia Street's otherwise tony "vintage" boutiques. Hit or miss, it's certainly worth a peek.

THE CATCH The limited opening hours make it difficult to catch this tiny store open, but it's certainly worth the effort.

St. Francis' Churchmouse Thrift Shop

2408 Ocean Avenue
(415) 587-1082

Wednesday, Thursday, Friday, and Saturday, noon to 4:00 P.M.

When you can find it open, this is a great place for some unexpected, dirt-cheap finds. It's what thrift store shopping should be—tiny, volunteer run, eclectic, and did I mention cheap? It was hard to find anything over $10, and considering the space, there's a good selection of women's and men's clothing, kids' clothes, toys, books, and the usual bric-a-brac.

THE CATCH Hours are limited.

FLEA MARKETS

Alemany Antiques and Collectibles Market
100 Alemany Boulevard
(415) 647-2043

Sunday, 7:00 A.M. to 3:00 P.M.

On Saturday this lot under the Interstate 280 overpass is a food and produce market. But on Sunday more than 250 vendors of everything under the sun—tools, serving platters, purses, toys, etc.—come out to peddle their wares at adjustable and solid prices.

Berkeley Flea Market
Ashby BART station parking lot (Ashby Avenue at Martin Luther King Jr. Way), Berkeley
(510) 644-0744

Saturday and Sunday, 7:00 A.M. to 6:00 P.M.

This is a beaut of the area—particularly because it's so easy to get here via BART from SF. The happy browser will find both good prices and vintage boutique heft—and if you make reasonable offers, you'll garner a bit of haggling power. Regular items include good quality handmade soap, an excellent selection of African art and clothing, mid-century furniture and furnishings, tube socks, and so very much more. Be sure to have lunch from the mobile van selling African food—delicious!

CHEAP CLOTHING

Aardvark's Odd Ark
1501 Haight Street
(415) 621-3141

Wasteland down the street wouldn't even think twice about peddling some dainty frock from a bygone era for $50, but here, old Aardvark's keeps prices on simpler clothes, like button-downs and jeans, a bit easier to digest. There are lots of men's clothes here, a rarity in Haight Street's many better secondhand shops, and lots of great costume pieces to choose from (like house-made smoking jackets and frilly flapper panties) that won't break the bank.

Buffalo Exchange

1555 Haight Street; (415) 431-7733

2585 Telegraph Avenue, Berkeley; (510) 644-9202

1210 Valencia Street; (415) 647-8332

www.buffaloexchange.com

This large national chain has a good selection of hipster clothing at somewhat erratic, reasonable prices—though beware of the recent trend toward throwing new stuff onto the racks as well, as $25 for a T-shirt is no bargain. If you own more stylish, seasonal clothes than you know what to do with, you can bring in your duds for cash money or store credit. Don't expect to get rich quick, however: They only buy great stuff in good condition that's right for the weather. It's worth a shot, but chances are you'll be schlepping your extras to the thrift store regardless.

Clothes Contact

473 Valencia Street
(415) 621-3212

Here the savvy shopper in touch with the rules of gravity will succeed: All clothes are $10 a pound, which makes it a boon for buyers of T-shirts, lingerie, and light cotton fabrics, and just a pretty good deal for that hefty three-piece fake fur suit (though there is a price ceiling in place for heavy winter coats and such). Come here not just for clothes but also for reams of vintage fabric, scarves, ties, and other cool, retro items in bulk.

Clothing Swap

www.clothingswap.org

Find five friends your size, invite them and their unwanted clothes to your house, dump everything in the middle, and let everyone take home new attire, carting the rest to the Salvation Army on the way home. Or if this is just too much work for you, and you're a woman living in the Bay Area, you can join the rest of the "divas" paying $25 to attend this much larger clothing free-for-all that adds the benefits of goody bags, cocktails, and sometimes snacks and entertainment. Even if you leave with just a couple of garments, it's still a good value for your money. Plus you get the motivation of cleaning out your closet and donating to a noble cause. Log on to the Web site and sign up for the next event near you.

THE CATCH

Joining the swap is $25.

Crossroads Trading Company

1901 Fillmore Street; (415) 775-8885

1519 Haight Street; (415) 355-0555

555 Irving Street; (415) 681-0100

2123 Market Street; (415) 552-8740

www.crossroadstrading.com

This national chain has locations peppered throughout SF. The clothes run on the smaller, more female, more stylish side, with heaps of "cute" accessories. Each locale caters a bit to the neighborhood. The Market Street/Castro venue carries more men's clothes, for example, and the Fillmore spot tends to have a higher concentration of career and designer clothes. For that hip, urban look, this is a great place to revitalize a boring wardrobe and save a few clams in the process.

Held Over

1543 Haight Street
(415) 864-0818

Great used hipster clothes and costume supplies in great condition for a great price. What's not to love? This Haight Street mainstay is a must-visit for the thin-walleted urbanite. Clothes are sorted by decade, so shoppers can achieve the look they seek, and there are lots of men's clothes, coats and jackets, pajamas, etc., motivated to move.

H&M

150 Powell Street
(415) 986-4215

What IKEA is to furniture H&M is to clothes, and ever since this Swedish bombshell descended upon Union Square in 2005, cheap-seeking, youth-oriented shoppers have been gobbling up these "fast fashions" for men, women, and children like a bowl of Swedish meatballs. New inventory pours in regularly, and most items in the mammoth, two-story discount department store are under $30—mere diddly for brand-spankin'-new, very "now" attire.

TIP Avoid the long lines and savage crowds on the weekends if you can.

Loehmann's

222 Sutter Street
(415) 982-3215

If you're female, skinny, and label conscious, you probably already know about this place, but just in case, we're here to share with you one of our best-kept secrets for new clothes on the cheap. What didn't move in major department stores across the country ends up here (or at any other of this national retailer's many locations), crammed onto racks sorted by designer, and surrounded by a never-ending drove of compulsive shoppers who would happily rip that Marc Jacobs skirt out of your hand. If you're looking to score below the ankles, Loehmann's Shoes is located across the street.

Mary's Exchange

1302 Castro Street
(415) 282-6955

This small, tightly packed Noe Valley storefront does a lot with a tiny amount of space. The focus tends to be on better vintage goods, some designer labels, and well-priced consignment with good turnover all around. Women's clothes only, with jewelry and other accessories.

Mission Thrift

2330 Mission Street
(415) 821-9560

Another great stop for great clothes, leaning heavily on T-shirts, tank tops, and simple, everyday clothes for the Mission dweller (or those who look like one). Don't bypass the dollar racks out front, as sometimes the finds are excellent. Though heavily bent toward women's fashions, with a good selection of purses, leggings, tights, and so on, it's also worth a stop for the guys.

Thrift Town

2101 Mission Street
(415) 861-1132
www.thrifttown.com

Make no mistake: It's got the name "thrift" in the title, but this is a for-profit enterprise. Despite this status, this locale of the national chain still boasts pretty good prices on great clothes for men, women, and kids; fantastic household items like towels, dishtowels, and bedding; and a whole floor of furniture upstairs that ranges broadly in quality but can be the site of some great archeological finds. The place is huge, with a high turnover, yet you'll usually walk out with something.

TIP

The tiny neighborhood newspaper, *Mission Dispatch*, frequently runs a coupon advertisement for $3 off any Thrift Town purchase of $10 or more. For your cheapskate convenience, copies of the newspaper can often be found on a newsstand at the front of the store near the check-out line.

GREAT NEIGHBORHOODS FOR
THE PENNY-PINCHING

Worth Avenue in Palm Beach and Rodeo Drive in Beverly Hills. Both signify what shopping in a neighborhood can deliver. The following are nothing like those two; they are simply cost-efficient solutions to acquiring the stuff that we require. Thus, here are some neighborhoods to peruse for cheap goods in San Francisco.

Inexpensive kitchen goods and housewares

Clement Street between Second and Ninth Avenues

Many shops featuring good pots and pans, cooking utensils, ceramic bowls and serving pieces, teapots, etc., many with a Japanese and Chinese aesthetic at excellent prices. This is a great place to buy gifts for others, such as pretty sets of ceramic tea accoutrements or lacquer bowls all boxed up and ready to give for as little as ten bucks. You'll find cheap brooms, mops, plastic buckets, garbage cans, clothespins and laundry bags; off-brand, black-market toothpaste and dishwashing soap; and other assorted sundries needed for everyday living.

Cheap new backpacks, luggage, and clothing

Mission Street between 20th and 26th Streets

Check carefully to make sure the quality level is adequate for the price—but at these prices, you shouldn't expect too much. There are backpacks and travel goods for vacationers and students, and this is one of the best places to pick up that Dora the Explorer or SpongeBob SquarePants backpack for the kids. Stock up on tube socks, cheap underwear for the whole family, and basic workout gear like sweatpants, hoodies, packaged T-shirts, and the like. Other items of note: a plethora of piñatas, fancy christening dresses for little girls, plastic flowers, and holiday decorations.

San Francisco souvenirs

Chinatown: Grant Avenue between Bush and Broadway

Of course this is a great neighborhood for picking up Mao hats, silky Chinese pajamas, and bamboo plants for supercheap, but this stretch of Grant is also the place for visitors to find that perfect piece of SF memorabilia to bring home for a song. T-shirts, coffee mugs, paperweights, postcards, and the like are plentiful and bargain bin, as are cable car replicas, calendars, baseball hats, and more. While you're here, shop for cool oddities like wind-up sushi, slippers with spangles, and children's toys galore.

CUT-PRICE BOOKSTORES

Anarchist Bookfair

www.bayareaanarchistbookfair.org

Though not the official site of the Anarchist Bookfair event, this shop will inform you of when the annual springtime happening takes place. Admission is always free, and browsing books cost nothing. Should you choose to purchase a few tomes, prices are kept low enough so that all workers can afford them. In addition to books, there's a host of free presentations and panels for the like-minded thousands of attendees.

Black Oak Books

540 Broadway Street; (415) 986-3872

630 Irving Street; (415) 564-0877

www.blackoakbooks.com

New, used, and antiquarian books abound, all in excellent condition, and all at good prices.

Dog Eared Books

900 Valencia Street

(415) 282-0213

www.dogearedbooks.com

The store is good sized but not mammoth, and yet the selection is so well honed we never walk out without something. Lots of paperbacks, including general fiction, biographies, and philosophy, at excellent prices, plus a fine selection of underground comic books, magazines, and even children's books for the liberal child.

TIP Don't miss the free book bin!

Friends of the Library Bookshops

Book Bay Main, 100 Larkin Street; (415) 557-4238

Book Bay Fort Mason, Fort Mason Center, Building C; (415) 777-1071

www.friendsandfoundation.org

Half a million books are donated to the public library each year, and these two outposts, open to the public, sell those that don't get logged into the stacks for as little as a dollar a piece. The selection is always changing—each month features a different theme or genre, listed on the Web site. Online shopping is also offered. Be sure to check the Web site for the one-day, 200,000-titles-strong Friends of the Library annual book sale, where everything is $1 or less.

THE CATCH Although the Fort Mason shop is much larger than its main branch counterpart, it is less conveniently located, and parking fees are charged.

Green Apple Books & Music

506 Clement Street

(415) 387-2272

Many people complain about the doing-you-a-favor service, but one thing cannot be disputed: This is one of the best-stocked, largest, oldest, and just neatest used book stores (and now, music, DVD, and video games, too) in the city. Plan to spend the day, because there's so much to look at, but with prices at roughly half the cover price, you won't have to spend a whole lot of cash to find something new to read.

TIP Don't miss the free book bin!

Magazine

920 Larkin Street

(415) 441-7737

Though this shop mainly specializes in highly collectible magazines pre-1960, the 35-cent table of more recent used periodicals fills a niche like no other, particularly if you can't steal that issue of the *New Yorker* or *Food & Wine* from your doctor's waiting room. Come to browse, to step into a time warp, or just to find something to read at a fraction of the newsstand cover price.

Needles and Pens

3253 16th Street

(415) 255-1534.

www.needles-pens.com

Cheap stuff to read doesn't just come in hardback from major publishing houses, ya know. For a dollar or two, you can widen your brain with do-it-yourself zines galore, small labors of pulp-reading love produced all over the country. They carry an excellent selection of them here, among other small-batch arts-and-crafts goods and community events, almost all of which are kept entirely affordable.

USED RECORDS STORES

Amoeba Music

1855 Haight Street

(415) 831-1200

www.amoebamusic.com

Mammoth, well-loved, and well-stocked Amoeba offers a boatload of cheese-laden vinyl on sale for a buck a piece, plus the best selection of used CDs in genres so plentiful you've probably never heard of half of them. Amoeba will also buy or trade your used tunes. This is a record store you could easily spend the day in and the kind of place that makes your out-of-town visitors wish they lived here.

Rooky Ricardo's Records

448 Haight Street

(415) 864-7526

All used, all the time. You should certainly expect to pay some top dollars for rare first pressings from this ample collection of 45s, but there are plenty of interesting finds in an affordable price range. This is browsing heaven for those who like to dabble around the turntable, and the vibe is pure local, friendly, and attitude free.

Streetlight Records

2350 Market Street; (888) 396-2350

3979 24th Street; (888) 682-3550

www.streetlightrecords.com

New, used, and barely abused audible media—such as vinyl, CDs, 45s, cassettes, and yes, even video discs—are bought and sold every day for pretty good prices going both in the door and out. This is a general-interest music seller, thus you're just as likely to find classical or bluegrass as the latest hip-hop or electronica.

CHEAP FURNITURE AND HOUSEHOLD MISCELLANY

Bernal Heights Annual Neighborhood Garage Sale

(415) 206-2140

www.bhnc.org

Every August

It's worth the legwork to discover the date of this mamma of all garage sales. Roughly 150 arty, affluent, city-savvy households and families clean out their storage spaces and sell what's not needed, and this is where the bargain hunter can seek, haggle, and score. Everything you can dream of is present and accounted for, from kids' stuff and yard supplies to furniture, clothes, bongs, and bongos—it's all ripe and ready to move. Get there early, and bring cash.

Crate & Barrel Outlet

1785 Fourth Street, Berkeley

(510) 528-5500

All the goodies that stock the shelves of this nationwide, giant home retailer—wine glasses, place mats, couches, chairs, pillows, rugs, and so on—show up here once deemed overstocked, discontinued, or damaged. Prices are slashed anywhere from 10 to 80 percent. True bargains for better-quality stuff can be had by the frequent and patient shopper.

EQ3 Modern Home Furnishings
540 9th Street
(415) 552-2626

Slushing down from the Great White North, this Canadian chain of low-priced, varying quality, stylish furniture for every room of the urban hipster home is a great place to find a couch when your friend flakes on a ride to the blue and yellow master of Emeryville. Desks, storage, tables, beds, chairs, and household accessories abound at eye-pleasing, relatively affordable prices.

IKEA
4400 Shellmound Street, Emeryville
(510) 420-4532
www.ikea.com

You hate it. You love it. You've seen the film *Fight Club* and desperately hoped that your own living room doesn't look quite so "IKEA catalog." But it's hard to resist the lure of this Swedish household retailer, which is a massive, reliable source of attractive, dirt-cheap, build-it-your-damn-self furniture for every room of the house with varying levels of quality. Don't forget that they can be cheaper than a thrift store for items like cups and plates, desk lamps, and candles, all chock-full of urban sensibility and good taste.

> TIP
> Avoid IKEA on the weekends if you can, as the swarm of nesting couples from all over the Bay Area can be too much to endure.

Mickey's Monkey
214 Pierce Street
(415) 864-0693

We can't imagine how they can continue to pay the rent with prices so low, but this Lower Haight longtime resident is a must-visit if you're looking for a new dresser for under a hundred dollars, plus a whole bunch of other well-maintained, kooky, retro household bric-a-brac, jewelry, bar sets, cool lighting, or whatever else tickles the Monkey's fancy this week. Better than junk, but still priced accordingly, their space limitations spill out onto the sidewalk and make it worth a visit.

San Francisco Public Utilities Commission Water Conservation

(415) 551-4730

www.sfwater.org (click on "water conservation")

The PUC really, really wants you to start saving water, and to motivate you (and your landlord) to do so, they've come up with a number of cash-incentive programs to get you to go with the low-flow. For starters, they will come to your home (for free) and assess your faucets and appliances and make suggestions on how you can do your environmental part. Then you can get subsidized household plumbing and appliances. For instance, they will sell you a lead-free faucet for just $10 (try finding that at Home Depot). And they offer rebates: up to $125 on ultralow-flow toilets or up to $150 on the purchase of a new, green washing machine.

NEED SOME CRAP?
VISIT SCRAP!

The Scroungers' Center for Reusable Art Parts

801 Toland Street

(entrance on Newcomb Avenue between Toland and Selby)

(415) 647-1746

www.scrap-sf.org

Better known as SCRAP, this is an absolutely indispensable nonprofit resource of cheap raw materials for school projects, art projects, Burning Man theme camps, or anyone who likes to make something out of almost nothing. Come here for unheard-of pricing on quality, donated textiles, paper, wood, buttons, carpet squares, and odd finds like matching band uniforms, plastic tubes, hundreds of doors, etc. They accept donations (though they're very picky about what they take in), and they teach workshops on how to get the most out of the materials that they offer, such as courses on binding your own books, marbling paper, and more. All prices are dirt cheap and negotiable—usually just a few dollars for a grocery-store bag full of materials.

{ HEALTH }
AND MEDICAL:
LIVE FREE OR DIE

"By sowing frugality we reap
liberty, a golden harvest."

—Agesilaus

Insurance? Are you kidding? At those prices? Even if you have the cheap plan, can you actually rely on it? Unless their employer is paying for health insurance, many city dwellers can't shell out the thousand smackers a month that it would cost to be protected—particularly when they're mostly healthy as an ox anyway. If you're among those without a health safety net, fear not, as there are many preventive services for physical and mental health to call upon before you head to the emergency room. Exercise, eat well, and take advantage of these sliding-scale or no-cost health-care opportunities. Most are open to everyone and don't have very-low-income restrictions, and using them doesn't take away services from the homeless or those truly in need.

MAJOR MEDICAL

Haight-Ashbury Free Medical Clinic
558 Clayton Street
(415) 487-5632
www.hafci.org

The name says it all. Serving more than 65,000 patients a year, this massive, long-standing sliding-scale health-care center strongly believes that medical attention is "a right, not a privilege." The clinic provides general health-care exams and advice, substance abuse programs, and referrals to other beneficial programs.

Huckleberry Youth Services at Cole Street Clinic (HYSCS)
555 Cole Street
(415) 386-9398
www.huckleberryyouth.org/cole.html

This clinic is a project of the University of California, the San Francisco Department of Public Health, and the Huckleberry House, a teen services organization. The clinic offers numerous types of physical care plus no-fee individual counseling, psychotherapy, and case management to teenage youth. Age-appropriate programs include birth control, HIV prevention, peer counseling, violence prevention, and more.

Lyon-Martin Women's Health Services
1748 Market Street, Suite 201
(415) 565-7667
www.lyon-martin.org

Since 1979 this kick-ass not-for-profit clinic has reached out to lesbians and other female populations with quality low-cost or no-cost health-care options, and now they serve 3,000 appointments a year. In addition to general health care, they cater to gynecological and hormone therapy, some fertility care, and vaccinations, immunizations, and other preventive care in English and Spanish.

Magnet
4122 18th Street
(415) 581-1600
www.magnetsf.org

Free sexual services for gay men, including sexually transmitted disease (STD) and HIV testing, as well as counseling services, hypnotherapy, and free Internet access in a stylish, intimate Castro setting. In addition, Magnet strives to be a community hub, hosting numerous events and mixers for new men in town.

North East Medical Services (NEMS)
1520 Stockton Street (main location)
82 Leland Avenue
2308 Taraval Street
(415) 391-9686
www.nems.org

Quality health care is provided in English and in a number of Asian dialects and languages, regardless of the patient's ability to pay. A staff of more than twenty physicians offers a wide range of services at three locations citywide, including pediatrics, optometry, podiatry, cardiology, and numerous aspects of curative and preventive health. Certainly it's not fancy, but the staff is thorough, accurate, and willing to work with anyone who is considered low income or uninsured.

Planned Parenthood Golden Gate

(800) 967-7526

www.ppgg.org

For birth control and all aspects of reproductive health services at a sliding scale, this national organization allows local residents to calculate the cost of their appointment on the Web site above, based on insurance coverage (or not), income, and services sought. A good amount of informative articles and other health information is available online.

San Francisco City Clinic

356 Seventh Street

(415) 487-5500

www.dph.sf.ca.us/sfcityclinic

Drop-in free and low-cost reproductive health services are offered to all patients, including info on STDs, condom use, lifestyle choices, and much more. This community project features a good amount of health information on its Web site for men and women of all ages.

San Francisco Free Clinic

4900 California Street

(415) 750-9894

www.sffc.org

No-fee medical services, including visits with specialists, are made possible by a busy team of 160 health-care providers who donate their time, medications, equipment, and funds. Visits are free, but donations are accepted.

THE CATCH
Patients cannot have medical insurance of any kind, and appointments for all services are required.

San Francisco General Hospital
1001 Potrero Avenue
(415) 206-8000

A project of the City and County of San Francisco and UCSF Medical Center, this full-service, acute-care hospital refuses no one, regardless of insurance or financial ability to pay. Payment is assessed by income. It is the only facility in SF to offer twenty-four-hour emergency psychiatric services. It also features a trauma center; children's, family, and women's health-care clinics; and general medical care.

Sister Mary Philippa Health Center
2235 Hayes Street, Fifth Floor
(415) 750-5517

This free clinic of St. Mary's offers hands-on medical care to thousands of patients each year, either free or at a reduced rate.

St. Mary's Medical Center
450 Stanyan Street
(415) 668-1000
www.stmarysmedicalcenter.org

This private Catholic hospital offers an impressive host of community outreach programs and health advice programs—simply click on the current Web site listings of classes and events. Lectures and roundtable discussions cover everything from health insurance counseling to living with diabetes. Community programs include free blood pressure screening and a mall walking program. Or check out the half-dozen support groups for bereavement, menopause, and more.

The Women's Community Clinic
2166 Hayes Street, Suite 104
(415) 379-7800
www.womenscommunityclinic.org

Free, respectful, quality health care is their guarantee for their women patients, as administered by the all-women staff. General women's health, gynecological exams, and screening for STDs are the bulk of their repertoire, along with pregnancy testing and community outreach. Services are offered for all women age twelve and above.

TALKING THERAPIES AND ALTERNATIVE HEALTH SERVICES

The Clinic of the American College of Traditional Chinese Medicine
450 Connecticut Street
(415) 282-9603
www.actcm.org

The primary goal of this learning institution is to treat the community to the best of its ability, and it claims to be able to assist with maladies including addiction, pain, emotional well-being, and respiratory and digestive health and maintenance. They offer special rates to seniors and students and a sliding scale for the income qualified. Modalities covered include moxibustion, tui na, cupping, nutritional counseling, acupuncture, herbs, and more.

Depression and Bipolar Support Alliance of San Francisco
(415) 995-4792
www.dbsasf.org

Young adults, friends, and families of the DBSA are welcome to attend peer support meetings at no charge. A $20 annual membership fee is requested, but no one will be turned away. Check the Web site for the current schedule and meeting location.

Intercounty Alliance of Alcoholics Anonymous Serving San Francisco and Marin Counties
www.aasf.org

Those wrestling with alcohol addiction can find resources here to help them stay clean and sober, including meeting schedules, contact information, and more.

Narcotics Anonymous San Francisco Area
www.sfna.org

Tune in to local meetings and events at this peer-sponsored local branch of the nationwide network.

Overeaters Anonymous of San Francisco
www.oasf.org

This self-help nationwide program's local chapter keeps an updated list of meeting information, tools to jump-start an overeater's recovery, some local contact info, and more.

Quan Yin Healing Arts Center
1748 Market Street
(415) 861-4964
www.quanyinhealingarts.com

A discount scale is offered for the uninsured, but a number of private insurances, including workers' comp, are accepted. Here patients, many of whom are chronically ill (though all are welcome), can come for treatment for whatever ails them through the channels of traditional Chinese medicine (TCM), meaning acupuncture, massage, herbs, qigong, and much more. The uninsured can buy a series of four acupuncture sessions at a significant discount. This is a nonprofit organization.

Reiki Center of the East Bay
5920 San Pablo Avenue, Oakland
(510) 653-9884
www.reikicentereastbay.com

Second and fourth Tuesday of the month, 7:00 and 8:00 P.M.

The low-fee clinic is run by volunteers who have been trained and are supervised at the clinic. It is designed for people who cannot afford private sessions (usually $70) or for those who cannot come during the regular workday hours. Call and arrange these low-fee sessions far in advance, as they tend to fill up quickly. Donations accepted.

San Francisco Sex Information

(415) 989-SFSI

www.sfsi.org

Monday through Thursday, 3:00 to 9:00 P.M.; Friday, 3:00 to 7:00 P.M.; Saturday, 2:00 to 6:00 P.M.

Honest, nonjudgmental, and frank information about all aspects of sex and sexuality are given out at no cost and anonymously via telephone (primarily) and e-mail. The Web site's excellent FAQs are likely to school any curious student of the subject.

{ OUTDOOR
FITNESS: }
THE AIR IS STILL FREE

"I believe that thrift is essential
to well-ordered living."

—*John D. Rockefeller*

As long as your lungs can pump and the rain stays at bay, San Francisco is your playground, your treadmill, and your gym. Just by walking outside nearly any day of the year, those seeking physical fitness will be greeted by temperate weather, stunning scenery, and enough hills to give even the staunchest athlete a decent reason to get hot and bothered. Think of this chapter as your personal trainer and workout coach, ripe with location-scouting suggestions to get you moving and your blood pumping. Take advantage of all that the sporting outdoors has to offer as only the Bay Area can grow it.

GREAT PLACES FOR A RUN OR A WALK

Cox Stadium
San Francisco State University campus, Nineteenth Avenue and Halloway

THE CATCH

Parking is widely available here, but you'll have to pay a buck an hour.

This track never closes, but your best bet is to show up any evening after 5:00, when all classes and sports teams have finished their practice for the day.

Kezar Stadium
Golden Gate Park (between Stanyan and Frederick Streets)

This is one of the most popular running tracks in the city. Even when it's crowded, there's still room for all, beginner and experienced runner alike.

Lake Merced Loop
Lake Merced, Skyline Boulevard, and the Great Highway

With more than 4 miles of waterfront, paved, and flat path, this is a fine spot for auto-free running, walking, dog walking, stroller pushing, etc. It's also near a giant mall, if that sort of thing is important to you.

Land's End, Lincoln Park, and Ocean Beach
Along the Great Highway

Couples have their wedding photos taken in front of the Land's End Palace of the Legion of Honor for good reason: The bay views are always breathtaking. Walk along the golf courses of Lincoln Park and the magic continues; you'll pass Seal Rock, the historic Cliff House, and the ruins of the lovely Sutro Baths along the way. Then the beach goes on—Ocean Beach, that is—and even the omnipresent fog of this Richmond District favorite cannot distract from its rapture and beauty.

Lyon Street Steps
Lyon and Green Streets

When your buns need a'crunchin', this is your Stairmaster au natural. The view is truly awesome, and the splendid homes that surround these posh digs are a sight to behold. Once you've made it to the top, you won't even notice that you're panting because the cityscape will take your breath away.

Marina Green and Fort Mason
Mason Street eastward to Aquatic Park at Beach Street

Start from the northernmost tip of the city and head east from the Golden Gate Bridge to the Marina Green and Fort Mason and continue eastward past Aquatic Park to Hyde Street Pier. The views are stunning, the paved expanse ample, and the inspiration to keep moving forward is strong. You can keep moving into Fisherman's Wharf, though the foot traffic of this tourist area may slow you down.

The Presidio and Crissy Field
Lincoln Boulevard to Lyon Street, Mason Street to Pacific Avenue
www.presidio.gov/experiences/trails.htm

This massive old military base is a lush, undeveloped Disneyland of the outdoors, full of tree-lined trails, miles of unhurried rolling avenues, and the Golden Gate National Recreation Area along the western, Lincoln Avenue seaboard. It connects with Crissy Field, a restored landscape with great bridge views, lots of cultural activities, and a great coffee shop (the Warming Hut) on premises.

PUBLIC POOLS

http://parks.sfgov.org

Fees are $4 per swim for adults, $1 for kids age seventeen and under, plus a dollar more for swimming lessons. Swim tickets are sold in books of ten for $34. Facilities include heated pools (usually eighty degrees), showers, changing areas, and lockers, although swimmers must bring their own locks. Lessons for children and adults are offered throughout the year, as well as water aerobics, water fitness, family swims, and lap swimming. Check the current schedule to see what's offered where.

Balboa Pool, *San Jose Avenue and Havelock; (415) 337-4701.*

Coffman Pool, *Visitacion and Hahn; (415) 337-4702. Scheduled to reopen in fall 2007.*

Garfield Pool, *26th Street and Harrison; (415) 695-5001.*

Hamilton Pool, *Geary Boulevard and Steiner; (415) 292-2001.*

Martin Luther King Jr. Pool, *Third Avenue and Carroll; (415) 822-2807. Two pools—a children's wading pool just 1½ feet deep, and another large pool for all.*

Mission Pool, *19th Street and Linda; (415) 695-5002. An outdoor pool open only in summer, usually May to October.*

North Beach Pool, *Lombard and Mason; (415) 391-0407. Two twin pools 90 feet long and 9 feet deep.*

Rossi Pool, *Arguello Boulevard and Anza; (415) 666-7014.*

Sava Pool, *Nineteenth Avenue and Wawona; (415) 753-7000.*

LOW-COST GOLF

San Francisco Municipal Golf Courses

http://parks.sfgov.org

The barrier to entry for low-cost golfing on one of SF's municipal courses may actually be more challenging than the game itself. Standard golf fees can hover near the $150 mark, truly keeping the sport's reputation as the pastime of the rich and powerful firmly on course. However, discounts are offered for many of the population in the checkered pants, including Northern California residents (around $100), seniors (around $60), juniors (around $20), and with a little legwork and persistent ingenuity, there are significant discounts offered to SF residents with valid San Francisco Recreation and Parks ID cards, with rates about a third of those of the general public. To get yours, show up in person at the treasurer's office, on the first floor of city hall, room 140, between 8:00 A.M. and 5:00 P.M., Monday through Friday. Note that applicants can only apply in person, and that these cards, annoyingly, cannot be issued at any golf course. Bring your state driver's license with SF address on it and one other piece of proof of your city residency, such as a utility bill, property tax statement, bank account statement, or any other recurring bill that has been received within the past ninety days. If your license does not have your SF address on it, you'll need two pieces of proof of residency. Pay $40. The residency card will be valid for discounts for a year, and it can be renewed by mail thereafter. The golfer in you will save up to $100 for every greens fee paid throughout the year.

THE CATCH: The city does not make obtaining a valid ID card easy.

Once you have your valid discount card, you are free to roam the rolling green at any of the following courses.

Golden Gate Park Golf Course

Forty-seventh Avenue and Fulton Street, Golden Gate Park
(415) 751-8987

This nine-hole "pitch and putt" is more for fun than for serious golfers, but it's easy to get to and a good choice for those just looking to get their driver wet. Summer camps for junior players are available—call for this season's offerings. No reservations are accepted; it's first come, first served.

THE CATCH: Residents pay $10; $12 Friday through Sunday.

Harding Park and Fleming Golf Courses

Skyline Boulevard and Harding Road

(415) 664-4690

Open to the putt since 1930, this course is surrounded by pretty Lake Merced. Its rolling hills have a certain amount of cachet, as the course is host to the annual San Francisco City Golf Championship (one of the oldest-running amateur golf events in the country) and other tournaments attracting the likes of Tiger Woods, making it the jewel in the city's crown. True, eighteen-hole Harding is pricey, but with your discount it's about a third less than regular fees. Nine-hole Fleming is a "pitch and putt" course, meaning it's halfway between clown's-mouth minigolf and a real course, making it a good choice for beginners.

THE CATCH Harding costs residents $46; $59 Friday through Sunday. Fleming costs residents $20; $22 Friday through Sunday.

Lincoln Park Golf Course

Thirty-fourth Avenue at Clement Street

(415) 221-9911

Stretching around Land's End along the water's edge with breathtaking views of the Golden Gate Bridge, this forested course's stunning vistas may distract your eye from the ball. This is also one of the courses used for the annual San Francisco City Golf Championships.

THE CATCH Residents pay $20; $24 Friday through Sunday.

TIP To make reservations for $1, call (415) 750-GOLF.

Sharp Park Golf Course

Sharp Park Road (off Interstate 280), Pacifica

(650) 359-3380

Just a few minute's drive from San Francisco to the south, this lovely day outing was originally landscaped in 1931 by John McLaren, the developer of Golden Gate Park. This 6,299-yard course sits alongside the Pacific Ocean and Laguna Salada, a natural lake ringed with plenty of flora and a variety of birds.

THE CATCH Residents pay $20; $24 Friday through Sunday.

TIP To make reservations for $1, call (415) 750-GOLF.

Other Golf Courses

Chuck Corica Golf Complex

1 Clubhouse Memorial Road, Alameda
(510) 522-4321

This incredibly popular conglomerate of the Earl Fry (18 holes, par 71, 6,141 yards) and Jack Clark (18 holes, par 71, 6,559 yards) Golf Courses offers challenging eighteen-hole championship courses as well as the MIF Albright Executive nine-hole course with a fully lit driving range. It's flat but very windy with numerous hazards. Still, there's plenty of space for big hitters to practice for distance.

THE CATCH

Residents pay $23; $27 Friday through Sunday. Rates drop to as low as $18 after 3:00 P.M. daily.

Gleneagles Golf Course

2100 Sunnydale Avenue (between Brookdale and Persia Street), McLaren Park
(415) 587-2425

THE CATCH

$14.00; $17.50 Friday through Sunday.

This expansive green is a nine-hole course tucked into the south of the city. It can be played as a serious eighteen-hole course, proving to be quite challenging.

Tilden Park Golf Course

Grizzly Peak and Shasta Road, Berkeley
(510) 848-7373

Here, the late bird catches the worm, as rates are deeply reduced after 3:00 P.M., and that can mean a hole-in-one of savings, particularly in the long days of summer. This picturesque East Bay golf attraction features eighteen holes within the woodsy Berkeley Hills, where you may putt among deer and other wildlife. Lessons are available at the on-site golf learning center.

THE CATCH

$30; $51 Friday through Sunday. After 3:00 P.M. the fee drops to $22; after 5:00 P.M. it's $15.

OTHER OUTDOOR FUN

Cal Sailing Club of Berkeley

124 University Avenue, Berkeley

www.cal-sailing.org

Check the Web site for the regular schedule of free open-house days, planned most frequently during summer. Members of this enthusiastic and generous sailing club volunteer their time and their boats to take landlubbers our for an enticing, membership-building traipse around the bay when the weather conditions are right (though there is no obligation to join the club). Guests should just show up anytime between 1:00 and 4:00 P.M. in warm, waterproof clothing, and children must be at least five years old. Bringing a change of dry clothes may be a good idea.

City Kayak

Embarcadero at Townsend, Pier 38

(415) 357-1010

www.citykayak.com

First Tuesday of the month

One of the best-kept secrets in water recreation, this beautiful and mildly challenging kayak tour captures the view from the other side of the ball park, the Bay Bridge, the Ferry Building, the Embarcadero, and more. And best of all, a certain number of seats for this monthly outing don't cost a thing—save for a gratuity for your tour guide. Registration for the free seats must be made in advance by signing up on the calendar section of the Web site. All gear, instruction, and guides are provided, but you should bring a change of clothes and shoes just in case you end up wet. This merchant asks that users just sign up and show up; please *do not* call the offices to inquire about this regular giveaway.

FREE TAI CHI IN SF PARKS

Sponsored by the San Francisco Neighborhood Parks Council and the Mayor's Office of Criminal Justice; (415) 621-3260; www.sfneighborhood parks.org/events/taichi.html. Check the schedule to confirm the current free offerings.

Bookman's Center, *446 Randolph; (415) 586-8020. Friday, 9:30 to 10:30 A.M.*

Golden Gate Park, *Senior Center, 6101 Fulton; (415) 666-7015. Beginners classes: Monday, 4:00 P.M.; Wednesday, 2:00 P.M. Advanced classes: Monday, 3:00 P.M., Wednesday, 1:00 P.M.*

Golden Gate Park, *Spreckels Lake, Thirty-sixth Avenue and Fulton. Saturday and Sunday, 8:30 to 9:30 A.M.*

Parkside Square, *Twenty-sixth Avenue and Vicente. Monday and Sunday, 8:00 to 10:00 A.M.*

Sunset Playground, *Twenty-eighth Avenue and Lawton. Monday and Sunday, 7:30 to 9:00 A.M.*

West Portal Playground, *the tennis courts at Taraval and Lenox Way. Friday, 11:00 A.M. to noon.*

Public Tennis Courts and Lessons
(415) 831-6302
http://parks.sfgov.org

Free courts and lessons

If tennis is your racquet, San Francisco boasts more than 132 free municipal tennis courts positioned near playgrounds, parks, and recreation centers, plus an additional 21 courts in Golden Gate Park that take reservations—but there is a fee involved for the privilege. Heavily trafficked Dolores Park may have you waiting forever for an open court, but in the city outskirts, such as at St. Mary's Recreation Center in Glen Park, the courts are ready for serves almost anytime.

Free beginning and intermediate classes for adults and kids are offered throughout the year. Students must bring their own racket, wear good tennis shoes, and donate a can of unopened tennis balls to play and learn. No drop-ins; reservations are required. The schedule of classes can be found on the Web site.

The San Francisco Lawn Bowling Club
Bowling Green Drive (near Sharon Meadow and the Carousel), Golden Gate Park
(415) 487-8787

Wednesday at noon; additional evenings in summer, or by appointment

One needn't be a white-clad septuagenarian to play the balls, but it would help if you want to fit in with this crowd. After watching members bowl their black orbs on the club's pristine expanse of green, bystanders have free weekly opportunities to try their own hand at the sport, with teachers who are always graciously willing to share the skills.

THE CATCH
Reservations are required for evening instruction, and flat-soled shoes are required.

Skateboarding in Crocker Amazon Park
Moscow and Italy Streets
(415) 337-4708
http://parks.sfgov.org

Helmets and protective padding are excellent ideas—almost as good as letting your teenagers or older kids thrash to their heart's content. This is the only official skate park in SF. It's free, and it is a scene unto itself.

{ INDOOR FITNESS: }
WORKING (IN) A WORKOUT

"An unhurried sense of time is in
itself a form of wealth."

—*Bonnie Friedman*

Let's face it: We love San Francisco's many twists and quirks, but the crummy winter weather—hell, even the crummy summer weather—can make any urbanite wonder why we left wherever it was that we migrated from. Despite the bouts of fog, cold, and rain, the body must move, but the expense of a gym membership can be so depressing that it might take a whole box of Twinkies to brighten our spirits. Fortunately, the flexible cheapskate with her ear to the ground will find that bargains, even in the realm of the indoor workout, can abound. Read on . . . and Twinkies be damned, you will learn how to tighten your wallet as well as your muscles.

FREE AND DISCOUNTED GYMS

ABADÁ-Capoeira San Francisco Brazilian Arts Center
3221 22nd Street
(415) 206-0650
www.abada.org

We cannot guarantee that you'll be spinning through the air in a split in the first thirty days, but it's worth a shot, and you're promised a guaranteed-to-sweat workout in the process. Brand-new adult students can purchase a discounted pass for four classes for $32, a substantial savings over the $12 drop-in fee. Regular class fees are slightly lower for kids under nineteen years old, and some financial assistance may be available for low-income youth.

THE CATCH

Cash or local checks only, and the $32 discounted pass must be used within thirty days.

Aikido Center

1755 Laguna Street
(415) 921-5073
www.pacific-aikido.org/sfcenter.html

Forget the one-time drop-in-and-taste approach to discipline and fitness offered by most gyms: Here beginning students have three weeks, at two sessions a week, to decide if aikido in Japantown is the right course of action to fit their lifestyle. At

THE CATCH } $9 sessions for three weeks.

just $9 a session, and with the flexibility to take the beginner's course as many times as you like, this is a license to stretch your physical as well as cultural muscles.

Berkeley Ironworks

800 Potter Street, Berkeley
(510) 981-9900
www.touchstoneclimbing.com

This East Bay cousin to the popular Mission climbing gym is larger and offers

THE CATCH } $10 before 3:00 P.M. weekdays.

a greater variety of workout classes, like cardio-kickboxing, core strengthening, yoga, kids' programs, and more. They also offer the same great price break for daytime climbers—just ten bucks before 3:00 P.M.

Curves

www.curves.com

At last count there were nine San Francisco locations of this women-only workout facility, plus plenty more scattered throughout the greater Bay Area, and 10,000 worldwide. Each is a franchise, thus the rules and policies may be slightly different, depending on which location you choose. Most offer some sort of no-obligation trial, either a week's free membership or a small handful of consulting sessions with a personal trainer. As with all gyms, expect a pretty hard

THE CATCH } Free trial membership . . . and membership pitch.

sell if you do indeed come in or give up your contact information. But if you're looking to get on some Nautilus machines gratis, this is your gateway.

Fight and Fitness

734 Bryant Street
(415) 495-2211
www.fightandfitness.com

THE CATCH $10 introductory fee for beginners for up to three classes.

It's not free, but where else can you try kicking some ass at Muay Thai, boxing, or mixed martial arts for adults and kids for $10? The gym will allow the introductory fee for up to three classes; beginners only.

Krav Maga

1455 Bush Street
(415) 921-0612
www.kravmaga-sf.com

If you've ever been interested in the kind of workout that can spout from an Israeli/CIA self-defense and fighting strategy, this is your chance to try it and not lose a single shekel. Call or send your contact info via the Web site, along with a good time to reach you, and they will sign you up for a free trial class and a free, celebrity-studded DVD. They also offer complimentary group training sessions for your group, corporate team, or nonprofit organization, covering the basics of self-defense and a fighting spirit.

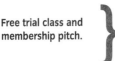

THE CATCH Free trial class and membership pitch.

Mission Cliffs

2295 Harrison Street
(415) 550-0515
www.touchstoneclimbing.com

If getting your butt in a sling and hanging off a rock is your idea of fun, then this indoor rock-climbing extravaganza is your mountaintop just ready to be summitted. Get here before 3:00 P.M. on weekdays and it's just $10 to drop in and climb, saving you $8 off the regular price paid by the after-work crowd. The first Friday of the month is women's night, and the third Friday night of the month is college student night. On both occasions, qualified attendees get in for just $10 (in the case of the students, valid ID is required).

THE CATCH $10 before 3:00 P.M. weekdays and on certain other occasions.

24-Hour Fitness

www.24hourfitness.com

This nationwide chain has eleven San Francisco locations, and they're sweetening the trap to help bring you into its well-toned folds: Sign up for either ten free days of gym membership or fifteen free days of workout classes and gym membership. Should you decide to join, the site offers other incentive programs, such as printable coupons to help you skip the initiation fee. Of course, none of this is possible without giving up your full contact info, so proceed with caution.

UCSF School of Medicine Classes in Tai Chi

1701 Divisadero Street, Suite 150
(415) 353-7718
www.osher.ucsf.edu/Classes/TaiChi.aspx

Beginning tai chi students, people over age fifty, and people with existing medical conditions all have options during this ten-week series of programs, and they're welcome to try the first class gratis. Should you decide this is for you, continuing your education is affordable—$90 for nine more sessions.

THE CATCH } Free first class; then $90 for nine sessions

FREE OR CHEAP YOGA

Bija Yoga Studio

1348 Ninth Avenue
(415) 661-9642
www.bijayoga.com

THE CATCH } Beginners get five classes for $50.

Compared with the usual drop-in fees, ten bucks per class for five classes is a bargain that will have any aspiring yogi or yogini breathing easier.

Integral Yoga Institute

770 Dolores Street
(415) 821-1117
www.integralyogasf.org

Pictures of the resident Sri Swami Satchidananda hang on the institute's wall, yet the yoga and meditation community they're seeking to build is entirely affordable. The regular hatha class drop-in fee is just $11, and always only $8 for those over age sixty-two, for those with HIV, and for first-time students. In addition, open meditation classes are offered daily. And on Tuesday and Friday, lunch can be had after the regular meditation session for just $5 (prearrangement required). Work trade for classes can also be arranged.

THE CATCH } Class fees begin at $8.

It's Yoga
848 Folsom Street
(415) 543-1970
www.itsyoga.com

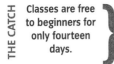

THE CATCH

Classes are free to beginners for only fourteen days.

Students new to this studio get a juicy two free weeks to try out the hot, steaming, ashtanga style of this SoMa studio. Just bring a towel—and the Web site coupon—to take advantage. Oh, and bring water . . . lots and lots of water.

Prenatal Yoga Classes
St. Luke's Hospital
3555 Cesar Chavez Street
(415) 824-0663

Saturday, 10:00 A.M.

Just show up—no experience or preregistration is necessary. Wear something comfortable, and let instructor Susan Arthur help moms-to-be relax and ease aching backs and hip joints in these free sessions.

Rusty Wells's Urban Flow
At ABADÁ-Capoeria Studios
3221 22nd Street
(415) 333-YOGA
www.rustywells.com

The entirely charismatic Rusty has a loyal following, so much so that this crowded room of pay-what-you-can regular devotees pays enough to keep him afloat. The suggested donation is a standard $15, but no one gives you the hairy eyeball as long as you put something in the donation box. Get there early, bring a towel and some water, and prepare to work on your body and breath. Call the phone number

THE CATCH

Suggested donation is $15.

listed above or check the Web site for his ever-changing schedule. Note that Rusty teaches many classes all over town, but only those at ABADÁ are donation based.

Sivananda Yoga Vedanta Center San Francisco
1200 Arguello Boulevard
(415) 681-2731
www.sfyoga.com

This global nonprofit center offers a wide variety of Eastern practices, including some ayervedic courses, vegetarian cooking, and meditation, but they're mainly known for their yoga for practitioners of all levels. Check the schedule and drop

THE CATCH

First class free; $10 thereafter, with bulk discounts available.

by anytime, as the first time you hit your mat is on the house! After that, regular drop-in classes are ten bucks a pop, with bulk discounts available.

The Yoga Loft

321 Divisadero Street

(415) 626-5638

www.theloftsf.com

New students can benefit from their first three classes at just ten bucks a pop (when

THE CATCH

Class fees begin at $10.

bought all at once), but existing students also qualify for rewards, such as an $11 student price and free classes for regular passholders when you bring a friend. Check the schedule for community classes, open to all, for $10.

Yoga Mob

www.yogamob.org

Taking it to the mat does not need to be a big-money affair, says this pioneering, grassroots team of practitioners. They hold classes irregularly and wherever space is available for use free of charge. Donation-based yoga is a mission and a revolu-

THE CATCH

Though the space costs nothing, the time of your instructor has some value. Donations are requested but not required. Please give what you can afford.

tion. Join forces with your fellow yogis and yoginis and learn to do the Cheap Bastards pose. Get on the mailing list to find the classes nearest you.

Yoga Tree

519 Hayes Street; (415) 626-9707

780 Stanyan Street; (415) 387-4707

1234 Valencia Street; (415) 647-9707

Yoga Flow Castro; 97 Collingwood; (415) 701-YOGA

www.yogatreesf.com

With four locations around the city, this mini local chain offers a wide variety of classes, instructors, and styles. For the student new to the Tree, they offer a substantial discount on your first handful of classes—three classes for $20—something

THE CATCH

Discounted fees for the first three classes or for off-hour community classes.

to be taken advantage of when contrasted with the $16-per-class regular drop-in fee. Check the schedule for off-hour community classes, where entry for anyone and everyone is just $8.

FREE YOUR MIND—MEDITATION THAT COSTS NOTHING BUT TIME

Brahma Kumaris Meditation Center

401 Baker Street

(415) 563-4459

www.bksanfrancisco.com

This local venue is connected to the group's 7,000 other centers in eighty countries, and as such it has the resources to offer a panoply of free classes, meditation sits, and retreats, some drop-in and some with reservations required. There's even "power" meditation and lunchtime sits in the Financial District for the busy but mindful, courses of study offered in Spanish, and courses specifically for women, men, and seniors. Check the schedule to find out what's currently on offer.

Insight Meditation Community of San Francisco

Starr King Room of the First Unitarian Universalist Church of San Francisco

1187 Franklin Street

(415) 994-5951

www.sfinsight.org

Sunday, 7:00 to 9:00 P.M.

This long-standing and active sangha (Buddhist community) offers weekly sits and dharma talks, a rotating schedule of monthly events for those new to meditation practice, and a monthly potluck dinner. Tap into this community to hear about affordable (though not free) courses, workshops, and more to help deepen the practice of the serious lay student.

Maharishi Enlightenment Center

465 California Street

4111 18th Street, Suite 10

1245 Ninth Avenue, Suite B

(415) 433-2488 (recorded information)

Six million people across the globe have tried transcendental meditation, and at any of these three locations serving the eastern, central, and western parts of SF, you can, too. Call and leave your contact information to schedule a free, sixty-minute introductory lecture on the practice and its history.

■ **WORTH THE TRIP**

SPIRIT ROCK

5000 Sir Francis Drake Boulevard, Woodacre
(415) 488-0164
www.spiritrock.org

To truly nourish your interest in vipassana/insight meditation, come to the source—a stunning getaway of rolling acreage tucked into the lush hills of west Marin County, roughly an hour and fifteen minutes north of the Golden Gate Bridge. Your first visit to the Monday-night sitting group and dharma talk, always an experience of quality spiritual education, is complimentary, leaving you with the regular $8 fee still in your pocket (though basket donations for the teaching are still accepted). Arrive early enough and those dollars can be put toward the $10, self-service, delicious vegetarian buffet that precedes the session.

Makor Or Jewish Meditation Center
323 Fourth Avenue
(415) 221-8736
www.makor-or.org

This conservative Jewish meditation center is a project of Congregation Beth Sholom in the Richmond, and it strives to provide a spiritual bridge between daily minyan services and other regular temple events. Look for a regular schedule of free morning and evening sits, usually forty minutes long, plus a rotating schedule of retreats, classes, and tools to help practitioners deepen their understanding of spirituality and the Jewish faith.

San Francisco Meditation Group

385 Ashton Avenue
(415) 584-8270
www.srf-sanfrancisco.org

This meeting group of the Self-Realization Fellowship, an organization founded by Paramahansa Yogananda in the 1920s, holds weekly meditation and reading sessions that are open to the public gratis.

San Francisco Shambhala Meditation Center

1630 Taraval Street
(415) 731-4426
http://sfshambhala.org

The schedule of this mindfulness-based worldwide style of Buddhist meditation changes; it's an excellent introduction to the practice and a great foundation to shape the beginner's mind. The center offers free midweek evening introductory sessions as well as Sunday morning open houses and Saturday daylong retreats open to the public and gratis (though their hope is to have interested parties join as members of their community to keep their organization afloat).

Weekly Vipassana Meditation

St. John's Episcopal Church
1661 15th Street (entrance on Julian Street, through the garden)
(415) 447-7761

Tuesday, 7:30 to 9:00 P.M.

The church is not the spiritual base but rather just a meeting place of this weekly Buddhist meditation community as led by teacher Howard Cohn. Practitioners sit for roughly forty minutes, take a short tea break, and then stay for a forty-five-minute dharma talk. There is no fee to attend, but a basket sits by the door to help cover the cost of the room rental and to collect funds to cover the cost of the teaching.

{ LEARNING AND LECTURES: YOU'VE GOT CLASS }

"Lack of money is no obstacle. Lack
of an idea is an obstacle."

–Ken Hakuta

One cannot put a value on the price of an education—but it's always better to learn something for free. Luckily, San Francisco is a locale dedicated to self-improvement and enrichment at every turn, and there is no shortage of low-cost and no-cost organizations and opportunities to school you for a song. From bike repair to gardening to violin lessons and to the intricacies of world politics, you and your brain have many avenues to explore that won't cost much more than the time it takes to sit and listen. Sharpen your pencils and grab a recycled notebook. We've got a lot to learn.

GENERAL LOW-COST LEARNING

Berkeley Adult School
1701 San Pablo Avenue, Berkeley
(510) 644-6130
http://bas.berkeley.net

Providing quality education since 1881, this unique public school for adults offers a host of classes to the public for free, including instruction in ESL, basic education courses, and high school diplomas. Classes for adults with disabilities and older adult classes are free. The general public is welcome to sign up for very-low-cost courses in subject areas designed to enrich the quality of life or career, including job and office skills, the arts and social sciences, theater and financial planning, and a whole lot more.

The Curiosity Guild
3824 Mission Street
(415) 839-6404
www.curiosityguild.com

From glass etching to jam making, growing herb gardens to running an eBay business, and a few CD exchanges and gallery tours in between, members of the loosely organized, bicoastal guild teach fun and mission-critical skills to one another and the public at regular monthly intervals for a reasonable fee—usually in the neighborhood of $25 or so. Check the calendar or their blog for a list of current events.

Richmond Village Beacon, a Program of the Richmond District Neighborhood Center
George Washington High School
600 Thirty-second Avenue, Interim Unit 1
(415) 750-8554
www.rvbeacon.org

This bustling community center offers myriad after-school programs for middle and high school students plus an impressive array of free life skills courses for young adults ages eighteen to twenty-five. Committed students have the opportunity to learn real hands-on job skills, cooking know-how, renter's rights, personal financial management, and much more to arm themselves with the knowledge they need to make daily life better. Those who successfully complete the courses often receive a retail cash incentive to help them put their newfound knowledge to good use, such as a gift certificate to a hardware store or an electronics store. Advanced registration is required.

San Francisco City College
50 Phelan Avenue
(415) 239-3000
www.ccsf.edu

At just $20 per credit unit for California residents, this full-service learning institution offers a wide array of classes at all hours of the day or evening for those seeking a college degree or simply their own personal fulfillment. Placement services and career counselors make it possible to learn a new career on the cheap.

Even if you're not a paying student, the school offers a full calendar through most of the year of interesting films, concerts, lectures, and more. Check the calendar to take advantage of this gold mine of free happenings.

STOP SPINNING YOUR WHEELS

A chain of local enterprises will teach you the fine, free art of bicycle repair, handling, and safety.

Missing Link Bicycle Co-Op
1988 Shattuck Avenue, Berkeley
(510) 843-7471
www.missinglink.org

Fix your own flat, build your own wheels, and understand the tao of brakes and gears. All classes are taught by this collective's incredibly seasoned panoply of professionals, and they're offered as a public service to anyone on two wheels.

Pedal Revolution
3085 21st Street
(415) 641-1264

Lecture and demonstration repair clinics are offered periodically, and regular attendees can learn the skills they need to keep their steed well-tuned and operating. Call the store to find out what they're teaching next.

San Francisco Bicycle Coalition
995 Market Street, #1550
(415) 431-BIKE
www.sfbike.org

Check the calendar to find the current schedule of bicycle safety classes designed for anyone who navigates SF's mean, car-hogging streets. Learn about safety equipment, proper hand signals, and more. Preregistration is required.

San Francisco Public Library
Various locations
(415) 557-4400
www.sfpl.org

Though there's a heavy emphasis on the weekly roster of typing, Internet usage, and computer skills, the giving tree of your local public library offers the occasional crafts course, guides to unraveling the enigma of city government, and education on how to get the most out of library resource materials, to name a few. Of course, these are your tax dollars at work. Don't think of these classes as just free. Think of them as already paid for.

ARTS AND SCIENCES

Ask a Scientist Night
At the Canvas Gallery
1200 Ninth Avenue
(415) 504-0060
www.askascientistsf.com

Why do scientists study monkeys? What's the skinny on forensic science, the future of the electric car, and what, exactly, does $E=mc^2$ mean? Come absorb the brain dump of this very popular monthly lecture series that puts real live know-it-alls in the various fields of science in front of a leisurely, knowledge-hungry cafe crowd. After the lecture you can show everyone how smart you are at the lengthy Q&A session.

THE CATCH
This is a free event, but it's held inside the large and bright art cafe. Prepare to pay for at least a cup of coffee if you plan to fill a seat.

CounterPULSE
1310 Mission Street
(415) 626-2060
www.counterpulse.org

The second and last Wednesdays of the month, this activist arts organization hosts an excellent lecture series for one and all. Come and learn about the city's fascinating untold liberal history, and get an insider's look at the local politics that shaped this town. These topics intermingle with subjects of a ecological nature, such as a local frog restoration project or the general greening of the city. Periodic film nights on local topics round out the repertoire. This arts organization also has an evolving calendar of very affordable classes in every aspect of performance.

THE CATCH
A $3 to $5 donation is requested, but no one is turned away for lack of funds.

Harvey Milk Photography Center

Harvey Milk Recreational Arts Building
50 Scott Street
(415) 554-9522
www.sfphotocenter.com (class schedule only)

The budding shutterbug inside you will be happy to learn about photographic composition, negative development, and the mechanics of photo printing—and to attend classes that cost a fraction of what you'd pay elsewhere. The use of the darkroom is also enlightening for your wallet—just $50 for six months of access. Total beginners and studio professionals are welcome, but all must attend a free midweek orientation in order to become a member.

THE CATCH }
Membership gets you the discount.

San Francisco Art Institute

800 Chestnut Street
(415) 749-4563
www.sanfranciscoart.edu

Are there any words more sweet and ethereal than "free and open to the public"? If you, too, get a little lightheaded at the phrase, and you enjoy opening your mind to an expanding world of experienced and cutting-edge artists in multiple formats, this regular series of artist lectures will surely round out the mind. The artists who show and screen at this acclaimed school's galleries have a chance to share their vision during informal, and complimentary, evening discussions.

San Francisco Comedy College

315 Sutter Street
(415) 921-2051
www.sfcomedycollege.com

Is it a free lesson or a sales pitch? You be the judge. Either way, those who preregister are permitted to attend a single, midweek evening of free lessons in what makes you, and the jokes that you tell, so darn amusing. And while your butt warms the chair, you'll learn more about classes at the college and what they can do to get you a stint on Letterman.

THE CATCH }
Preregistration gets you the free lesson.

Sharon Art Studios

Golden Gate Park Children's Playground
(415) 753-7004, (415) 753-7006
www.sharonartstudio.org

Adult and youth arts and crafts classes are offered at excellent prices, as subsidized by the San Francisco Recreation and Parks Department. For as little as $40 for an eight-week kids' course, or $85 for a ten-week adult course, students can unleash their left brain on ceramics, lead glass, metal work, enameling, drawing, watercolor, and more. Short of studying the work of graffiti artists in the streets, this is some of the most inexpensive arts education available.

THE CATCH }
Additional material fees and studio fees may be required for some classes.

Terra Mia Decorative Art Studio

1314 Castro Street
(415) 642-9911
www.terramia.net

This underrated ceramic arts studio already has low prices—just $10 for unlimited use of the facilities for an entire day, and half price for kids. However, first-time customers who know their way around a keyboard and a pottery wheel can print out an online coupon and save a few bucks with a 20 percent off Web coupon and other specials. Returning clay slingers should check their monthly calendar for periodic free days and two-for-one specials.

THE CATCH }
$10 for facilities use per day, with some special discounts available.

FOOD AND WINE

Bartending School of San Francisco

760 Market Street
(415) 362-1116
www.sfbartending.com

The first three-and-a-half-hour class is totally free to those who register in advance, and serious students can even apply this education toward a completion certificate in bartending. Of course the school hopes that those who show up at one of these freebies will sign on to complete the course in its ten full sessions, but there is no obligation. Students will learn the proper mixology behind sixteen different elixirs. And no, drinks will not be served.

THE CATCH }
First class is free.

City College of San Francisco's Continuing Education Courses on Wine and Food

Fort Mason Art Campus
Laguna Street and Marina Boulevard, Building B
(415) 561-1860
www.ccsf.edu

The cooking classes here—everything from the knowledge of cupcakes to cheese tasting and appreciation—are a bit cheaper than most other one-day courses through retail chains, usually around $50 or so for an evening, but not a mammoth bargain. The real surprise and savings from this school for the rest of us comes from the wine courses, usually costing under $100 for a four-week session. The budding sommelier will be hard pressed to find a wine appreciation course at any comparable cost. Check this semester's course catalog for what's ripe on the vine.

THE CATCH
Classes aren't free, but the wine courses are a bargain.

CUESA Market to Table Events

Ferry Building Farmers' Market
1 Ferry Building, Suite 50
(415) 291-3276
www.cuesa.org

Saturday morning

The Center for Urban Education about Sustainable Agriculture serves up a delicious weekly menu of lectures, demonstrations, and informative cook-offs that showcase the best of seasonal foods and the best culinary talent of the Bay Area culinary elite. In addition to their monthly fetes like the Asparagus Festival or a celebration of mushrooms, local chefs detail everything from holiday cookie ideas to Iron Chef tomato. The patient and intrepid can linger afterward for a taste of what was prepared before their eyes. Get the newsletter to be kept abreast of other periodic events, such as free author readings with a food theme, local farm tours, and more.

Tuk Tuk Thai and Asian Market

1581 University Avenue, Berkeley
(510) 666-1120

Saturday, 3:00 to 4:00 P.M.

This Asian foods market already features a delectable and inexpensive selection of fresh foods that are ready to eat. But should this still prove too pricey, here's your even cheaper option: Show up for the free weekly cooking class, watch how one of your new favorite Thai dishes is prepared, and then stick around for very generous "samples" (i.e., late lunch) of whatever was wok-fried before your eyes. At our last visit, this wonderful East Bay free dining opportunity was quite poorly attended, meaning many more samples for us. . . .

MEDIA

The Long Now Foundation

Fort Mason Center, Landmark Building A
(415) 561-6582
www.longnow.org

What Slow Food is to the culinary arts, Long Now is to philosophy and thought. Brian Eno's pet project, this organization hosts a monthly lecture series that focuses on a different meaning of "here" and "now" as they pertain to a broader, slower scope of thinking. The speakers challenge attendees to ponder their personal responsibility when they consider the world, and this popular lecture series reflects this genre of thought.

THE CATCH: A $10 donation is requested for each attendee, but "it is certainly not required for attendance." Also note that because the lectures are unticketed, seats tend to disappear quickly.

Media Alliance

1904 Franklin Street, #500, Oakland
(510) 832-9000
www.media-alliance.org

The old, gray-bearded workhorse of the alternative media scene provides a slew of resources for the budding and seasoned journalist, including a job file, courses in everything from ethics to editing, and speaker events with the top names of the left-wing brigade. All of this costs money to produce, but it is also made possible by the sweat equity of its supporting community, and this could mean you. Simply work a set number of hours in exchange for partaking in what this well-versed organization has to offer. Contact them for more information.

THE CATCH: Work as a volunteer to attend programs for free.

World Affairs Council
312 Sutter Street
(415) 293-4600
www.itsyourworld.org

President Carter, Wesley Clark, and Willie Brown have all stepped into the ring of this international organization. It hosts 200-plus events per year that invite discussion on local, national, and international politics and topics. You, too, opinionated newshound, are welcome to join their ranks at any of their regular discussion platforms, including meetings exclusively for young adults, library lectures, school and corporate programs, and more. Many gatherings are free, many more are free to members, and those that do charge an admission fee tend to be affordable, in the $5 to $15 range. With attendance, those interested in political tectonics and socioeconomic shifts cannot help but learn more about their world. Check the current calendar for what's happening this month.

SPIRITUALITY

Bureau of Jewish Education Jewish Community Library
1835 Ellis Street
(415) 567-3327, ext. 703
www.bjesf.org/events.htm

From genealogy to Jews in the Jazz Age, a number of free talks and community events are held here in collaboration with the excellent library resources. They showcase Judaism not just from a religious perspective but from a thriving, modern, living point of view. All events welcome the general public to simply drop in and learn. The handful of events offered monthly changes often; consult the Web site to see what's on now. For those seeking more information on the nuts and bolts of the religion, find out when this year's Feast of Jewish Learning takes place. This is an outreach program for anyone wishing to learn more about Jewish education and practice.

TIP Free parking is available at the Pierce Street entrance.

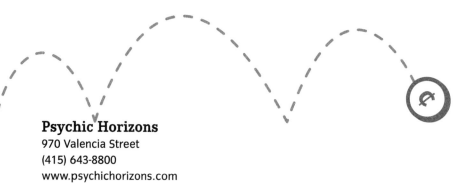

Psychic Horizons

970 Valencia Street
(415) 643-8800
www.psychichorizons.com

In the tradition of mediation and self-help workshops, this school and psychic reading center has been in the neighborhood for twenty years, and it continues to attract an interested (and interesting!) crowd. Tuesday night drop-ins are a way to meet staff and students and begin exploring your own psychic potential. Free, periodic weekend clinics offer readings and healing sessions as a way for students to practice the craft they study. There are also coupons galore on the Web site for healing and clinics to be scheduled at any time.

Yoga Society of San Francisco

2872 Folsom Street
(415) 285-5537
www.yssf.com

Those with more spirit than disposable income will find a host of free holistic opportunities, such as complimentary daily fire ceremonies and meditations. Check the calendar for regular monthly work days (when volunteers are given a vegetarian lunch in exchange for their good karma) and also periodic "yoga days," featuring an entire day of free instruction at no cost (though donations are welcomed).

BUSINESS AND FINANCIAL

Computer Workshops at the Apple Store
1 Stockton Street
(415) 392-0202
www.apple.com/retail/sanfrancisco

Mac users, rejoice! The Union Square flagship store features a full calendar of nearly a dozen daily courses designed to broaden and sharpen your Mac user skills. From pros to beginners, there are educational opportunities designed for all, at no cost, with no obligation to buy a thing. It's first come, first served (and seats can go quickly, especially on the weekend) for classes in GarageBand, podcasting, high-definition filmmaking, wireless networking, and much more. Drop in and make retail sing for its supper.

Foundation Center
312 Sutter Street, Suite 606
(415) 397-0902
http://foundationcenter.org/sanfrancisco

Though primarily geared toward serving the grant-seeking needs of the nonprofit sector, individual grant seekers can take advantage of this esteemed organization's generous resources to help draw attention and cash money to your personal philanthropic venture. Register for one of the free, regular courses in how to find funding, how to write a grant proposal, and how to target organizations that are most likely to fund your project. Learn how to use the excellent library of resources, a valued tool in the philanthropic community for fifty years.

Green Skills Job Training Program
(415) 206-9710
www.alivinglibrary.org

Low-income residents and new immigrant populations are encouraged to sign up for job training programs in marketable, hands-on skills, including alternative energy installation, gardening and landscaping, ecological restoration, ESL training, and basic computer use. Adults ages eighteen to twenty-four are eligible, and all classes are sponsored by Life Frames, Inc., and A Living Library, a nonprofit organization devoted to adding more life and greenery to the environment.

San Francisco Women on the Web

www.sfwow.org

This networking organization offers great grassroots networking via the popular Scrappy Hour—a male and female mixer for anyone interested in meeting more people in the technology industry, where the only thing you need to pay for are the business cards in your pocket and the drink in your hand. Women in the field will want to take advantage of the popular and chatty mailing list, the intimate (and free) Coffee Klatch roundtables, and the low-cost classes in programming.

Small Business Administration of San Francisco

455 Market Street, Sixth Floor
(415) 744-6820
www.sba.gov/ca/sf

From basic bookkeeping to accepting credit cards for your online business, the classes at this government-sponsored organization's local leg teach real and helpful skills for the enterprising individual—free or at subsidized fees. There are even classes in effective time management, and who couldn't benefit from that? The monthly, one-, and two-session classes change often. See what's on schedule to help your business, or your business idea, grow. Note that courses are taught in English and Spanish.

HEALTH AND WELLNESS

Bay Area Wilderness Training

300 Broadway, Suite 28
(415) 788-3666, ext. 122
www.bawt.org/train/skill_builders.php4

While this organization's main goal is wilderness leadership training for youth, it offers several community programs a month to boost the knowledge of any backwoods backpacker. Build your skills in the great outdoors by taking advantage of the free course offerings about aspects of first aid, including bandaging and splintering, and patient assessment.

TIP Graduates of their training courses are allowed to borrow BAWT's wilderness camping gear for free. Details are available on the Web site.

GREEN ENERGY

We need not burn through the environment. If you want to be more conscientious but aren't sure how to do it, these resources will show you that it's easy to be green.

Building Resources
701 Amador Street
(415) 285-7814
www.buildingresources.org
Artists and contractors alike will revel in this incredible hands-on resource in green building and clean living through recycled materials. The free course offerings at various Bay Area locations are a tremendous resource, and for just a few dollars in materials fees, they will teach you the likes of lamp building, environmental education and landscaping, and more. Once you have the know-how to use their vast inventory of recycled materials, they will provide you with the goods to launch your new project, including plywood, tile, wood, and bricks on sale at reasonable, community prices.

PG&E Classes in Energy Efficiency
851 Howard Street
(415) 973-2277
www.pge.com/education_training/classes/energy_efficiency/index.jsp#classresults
Pacific Gas & Electric sells the power, yet ironically it's willing to provide the general public with information to help people use less. In addition to its free classes for contractors and building professionals, PG&E offers up the latest thinking on topics like solar power, green building, and photovoltaic systems design.

THE CATCH
Registration is required, and classes seem to fill up fast.

TIP
If the SF courses are packed, students can try to enroll in courses in Oakland, San Jose, Concord, and elsewhere—including online.

Lunchtime Lecture Series at the Osher Center
1701 Divisadero, Suite 150
(415) 353-7700
www.osher.ucsf.edu/Classes/Lectures.aspx
Second Thursday of the month, noon to 1:00 P.M.

Anyone seeking to broaden his or her knowledge of mental affirmations in health care and alternative modalities is welcome to attend these free informal and informative lectures hosted by the University of California's School of Medicine. Vipassana meditation, jin shin jyutsu, and other topics are explored, including their positive effects when used in collaboration with traditional Western medical practices. Attendees are asked to bring their own brown bag lunch and eat while they learn. No preregistration is required.

Neighborhood Emergency Response Team Training
Sponsored by the San Francisco Fire Department
(415) 970-2022
www.sfgov.org/site/sfnert_index.asp

After the 7.1 earthquake that shook the city in 1989, this intensive, free course in how to survive and sustain the next natural disaster set out to educate the public with widespread success. Today, all are welcome to sign up and learn how to help themselves and their community when disaster hits the fan next time around. At prominent locations all over San Francisco, residents are just six sessions away from being a local hero and learning critical skills like how to wield a fire extinguisher, how to shut off the gas, search and rescue techniques, how to pack a survival kit, and much more.

San Francisco Sex Information
(415) 989-SFSI
www.sfsi.org

If you can say "sphincter," then you can say "SFSI." But no matter how you pronounce it, this thirty-year-old free service has the same goal: dispensing free, nonjudgmental, and anonymous sex and sexual health information via telephone and e-mail to anyone who asks—even those outside of the Bay Area. The main way to reach out and touch them is via telephone, but they offer limited hours; usually only late afternoons. Note that wankers need not apply.

GARDENING

Garden for the Environment

780 Frederick Street
(415) 731-5627
www.gardenfortheenvironment.org

Free and very-low-cost courses will teach you how to grow edible and environmentally harmonious plants. Learn the basics of everything from nuturing fruit trees to winter pruning to using recycled materials in your home garden. Several classes are offered every month, and no one will be turned away for lack of funds.

THE CATCH } Preregistration is required for the popular and celebrated courses, and some materials fees may apply.

San Francisco Garden Resource Organization (SFGRO)

P.O. Box 170396, San Francisco 94117
(415) 235-4292
www.sfgro.org

Free composting workshops and more are offered by this nonprofit, green-thumbed organization.

{FREE}
(THE) MEDIA

"Money is of no value; it cannot spend itself. All depends on the skill of the spender."

—*Ralph Waldo Emerson*

Last we checked, reading and listening are still free, and San Francisco's overeducated community offers about a zillion resources to help you master the intricacies of the world around you, whether it is local art happenings, politics, health care, or the beauty of the esoteric and obscure. Choose your method—print, airwave, etc.—and soak it all in. Anyone with an attention span can stay informed, educated, and independent of the corporate media giants that have come to dominate the industry. Here are a few of SF's best free "classrooms" to get you started.

LIBRARIES: FREE ACCESS

Public Libraries

Main Branch, 100 Larkin Street; (415) 557-4400; www.sfpl.lib.ca.us

Branch Libraries

Anza, 550 Thirty-seventh Avenue; (415) 355-5717

Bayview/Anna E. Waden, 5075 3rd Street; (415) 355-5757

Bernal Heights, 500 Cortland Street; (415) 355-2810

Chinatown, 1135 Powell Street; (415) 355-2888

Eureka Valley/Harvey, 1 José Sarria Court (16th Street near Market); (415) 355-5616

Excelsior, 4400 Mission Street (at Cotter); (415) 355-2868

Glen Park, 653 Chenery Street; (415) 337-4740

Golden Gate Valley, 1801 Green Street; (415) 355-5666

Ingleside, 1649 Ocean Avenue; (415) 355-2898

Marina, 1890 Chestnut Street; (415) 355-2823 (scheduled to reopen in summer 2007)

Merced, 155 Winston Drive; (415) 355-2825

Mission, 300 Bartlett Street; (415) 355-2800

Mission Bay, 960 4th Street; (415) 355-2838

Noe Valley/ Sally Brunn, 451 Jersey Street; (415) 355-5707 (closed for renovation until fall 2007)

North Beach, 2000 Mason Street; (415) 355-5626

Ocean View, 345 Randolph Street; (415) 355-5615

Ortega, 3223 Ortega Street; (415) 355-5700

Park, 1833 Page Street; (415) 355-5656

Parkside, 1200 Taraval Street; (415) 355-5770

Portola, 2450 San Bruno Avenue; (415) 355-5660

Potrero, 1616 20th Street; (415) 355-2822

Presidio, 3150 Sacramento Street; (415) 355-2880

Richmond/Senator Milton Marks, 351 Ninth Avenue; (415) 355-5600

Sunset, 1305 Eighteenth Avenue; (415) 355-2808

Visitacion Valley, 45 Leland Avenue; (415) 355-2848

West Portal, 190 Lenox Way; (415) 355-2886 (closed for renovation since 2004)

Western Addition, 1550 Scott Street; (415) 355-5727 (closed for renovation until fall 2008)

Public Library Bookmobiles

Branch Library Improvement Program Bookmobile, (415) 557-4343; call for schedule

Children's Bookmobile, (415) 557-4344; Monday to Thursday only; call for location schedule

Marina, Corner of Chestnut Street and Buchanan Street

Noe Valley, 665 Elizabeth Street in front of St. Philip School (near Elizabeth and Diamond)

Seniors' Bookmobile, (415) 557-4345; Tuesday to Friday only; call for location schedule

Sunset, Eighteenth Avenue between Irving and Judah at the Jefferson School white zone

West Portal, Claremont Boulevard at Allston Way

Western Addition, Corner of Post and Steiner Streets, beside Hamilton Recreation Center

Other Libraries

Barnett-Briggs Medical Library

San Francisco General Hospital Medical Center
1001 Potrero Avenue, Building 30, First Floor
(415) 206-3114
http://sfghdean.ucsf.edu/barnett/default.asp

Only staff and faculty can check materials out of the library, but the public is welcome to come learn, browse, and make copies to their heart's content. The library shelves 3,000 medical books and subscriptions to more than 300 current medical journals. Take advantage of librarian-guided use of online databases and special collections on bioterrorism, the flu vaccine, SARS, and other subjects.

Bureau of Jewish Education Jewish Community Library

Main location: 1835 Ellis Street (on the campus of the Jewish Community High School of the Bay); (415) 567-3327

Jewish Community Center location: 3200 California Street; (415) 292-1254

www.bjesf.org/library.htm

Holding more than 20,000 books, DVDs, CDs, and other media that chronicle every multifaceted angle of Judaism and Jewish life and culture, these two library locations foster book groups, community and arts events, lectures, and many more free events.

California College of the Arts Libraries

Simpson Library, 1111 8th Street; (415) 703-9574

Meyer Library, 5212 Broadway, Oakland; (510) 594-3658

http://library.cca.edu

If you're seeking inspirational imagery or want to brush up on the arts, perhaps the combined collection of 53,000 books, 12,000 periodicals, 2,000-plus videos, and about 160,000 slides will give your left brain something to work with. Meyer is the main branch and likely of most use, as it's the college's oldest, predating the SF branch by about eighty years. The public cannot take materials out, but copies are just a dime, and you're welcome to browse freely.

California Historical Society's Research Collections

678 Mission Street
(415) 357-1860
www.californiahistoricalsociety.org

From the early explorations of the state to events of the present day, this tremendous collection of photographs, manuscripts, maps, and historical texts is made available to all who seek it. The society boasts 35,000 printed materials plus thousands of images in entertaining and old-timey formats. Bonus find: A historical collection of street images, listed by name, is a great way to look into SF's colorful past.

THE CATCH

The collection offers only limited drop-in hours—Wednesday through Friday, noon to 4:30 P.M.

California Pacific Medical Center's Health and Healing Library
2040 Webster Street
(415) 600-3681
www.cpmc.org/services/ihh/hhc/ihhlibrary

The hospital claims that this is one of the largest public health and medical libraries in the country, and it has been in the information circulation business since 1981. Anyone seeking data on health and well-being, whether that be traditional Western studies or complementary medicine, is welcome to learn from the vast collection of 5,000 titles, videos and audiotapes, and computer access to scores of recent studies and medical journals. On the third Thursday of the month, from 10:00 to 11:00 A.M., anyone can take advantage of a librarian-led orientation on how to use the library's holdings most efficiently.

Center for Sex and Culture Library
398 11th Street
(415) 255-1155
www.centerforsexandculture.org

Though not a lending library, this fairly new facility, begun only in 2005, is building a browsable collection of pulp erotica, thesis and academic work on sex and sexuality, textbooks, and more—about 2,500 items at last count. The mission of

THE CATCH   This library does not offer drop-in hours at this time. Call to schedule an appointment to see the collection. Free, but donations are accepted.

this umbrella organization is to facilitate the study of sexuality and eroticism, thus most reasonable requests will strive to be fulfilled.

Helen Crocker Russell Library of Horticulture
San Francisco Botanical Garden at Strybing Arboretum
1115 Irving Street
(415) 661-1316
www.sfbotanicalgarden.org

With 27,000 volumes and 450 garden periodicals sprouting from its fertile soil, this free horticultural library, open since 1972, is an invaluable resource for any enthusiast with a green (or black) thumb. It's open seven days a week. You can drop in anytime to try to find solutions to queries on pest management, garden design, ethnobotany, and much more.

Holocaust Center of Northern California
121 Steuart Street
(415) 777-9060
www.hcnc.org/library.html

Though entirely a nonlending library, this research facility is pleased to make available for browsing and study its collection of texts on Nazi theory and occupation; liberation; war trials; Holocaust history, archives, and denial; and Jewish life in Europe before the Holocaust. Many resources and trial transcripts exist in twelve languages.

Holt Labor Library

50 Fell Street
(415) 241-1370
www.holtlaborlibrary.org

Labor activists and the public at large are welcome to utilize this noncirculating historical collection of the political and social movement, including 4,500 books (with an emphasis on Trotskyism); thousands of pamphlets, flyers, and brochures; current and historical periodicals; and other media that carry the message, including videos and DVDs.

THE CATCH
Appointments to view the collection are recommended.

J. Paul Leonard Library, San Francisco State University

1630 Holloway Avenue
(415) 338-1854
www.library.sfsu.edu

The public is welcome to view this extensive university's collections for free, but if you want to check something out, or take advantage of a host of other library features and services, you must be a paying member. This facility also offers a rich map and atlas collection and a large special collection on the labor movement and labor activity.

THE CATCH
$45 a year to become a Friend of the Library; call (415) 338-2408 or visit www.library.sfsu.edu/general/fol.html for complete instructions and a list of borrower restrictions.

J. Porter Shaw Library

At the San Francisco Maritime National Historic Park
Fort Mason Center (Buchanan Street and Marina Boulevard), Third Floor, Building E
(415) 561-7080
www.nps.gov/archive/safr/local/lib/libtop.html

This 17,000-foot facility is primarily a place to study, but it's certainly not without its charms for the seafaring fans of Pacific maritime history among us. The Shaw Library boasts two oral history/sea chantey listening rooms for the audio collection of a thousand-plus, plus facilities for viewing film and videos. Print materials include a hundred years of all of the local newspapers, vessel registries, more than 32,000 volumes, and photocopying services. None of their material leaves the premises, but it's free to look.

Prelinger Library

301 8th Street, Room 215

(415) 252-8166

www.prelingerlibrary.org

This private collection, for now still open to the public at no cost, is an impressive general interest resource of books, ephemera, and periodicals. Its charms come from its unique organizational structure that welcomes browsing and throws Dewey Decimal to the curb. Subject areas are simply limited to the four areas of landscape and geography, media and representation, historical consciousness, and political narratives beyond the mainstream. They specialize in the weird and the off-center and take pride in serving an imagecentric, wordsmithing, and artistic clientele. Note that this is a labor of love, and that drop-in hours can change suddenly and without warning. It's smart to check the current schedule before a visit.

Public Library of Science

185 Berry Street, Suite 3100

(415) 624-1200

www.plos.org

This nonprofit collection is mission driven by physicians and scientists to make widely available recent works of scientific and medical literature. You can visit the physical street location for free—but everything they publish is available, worldwide and with attribution, through their Web site.

San Francisco Law Library

401 Van Ness Avenue, Room 400 (main library and main location); (415) 554-6821

685 Market Street, Suite 420; (415) 882-9310

400 McAllister Street, Room 512 (San Francisco Courthouse); (415) 551-3647

www.sfgov.org/site/sfll_index.asp

Everyone should have free access to the materials they need to protect their legal rights, and this city-run facility strives to provide those tools to all who seek them. Not only will the staff teach you how to research difficult topics, such as docket research and local municipal code, but they also provide aspiring legal eagles with online and on-site librarian assistance and a plethora of digital database resources. Geared toward a lay audience, the awesome self-help page is a great resource for those beginning to navigate a course in the legal system.

San Francisco Performing Arts Library and Museum

401 Van Ness Avenue, Veteran's Building, Fourth Floor

(415) 255-4800

www.sfpalm.org

The SFPALM collects and makes available historical documents that chronicle performing arts in the Bay Area and beyond from the gold rush to the present. They boast over two million items of various media in their archives, including items from the San Francisco symphony, opera, ballet, and much more. They are a nonprofit organization with roots going back more than sixty years, and today, in addition to their physical holdings, they offer a host of events and exhibitions, for pay, that showcase themed aspects of their collection.

Sierra Club's William E. Colby Memorial Library

(415) 977-5506

www.sierraclub.org/library

This noncirculating reference collection is searchable either online or at its SF location, which is chock-full of books, periodicals, mountaineering journals, government documents, historic photographs, slides, maps, and memorabilia.

THE CATCH

Access is free, but appointments are a must.

Sutro Library, a Division of the California State Library

480 Winston Drive

(415) 731-4477

www.lib.state.ca.us

Though mainly a research tool serving Sacramento-area government officials, our local location contains genealogical and family history imagery and documents for all fifty states, including local history, and rare book and manuscript collections formed by Adolph Sutro. Any information from any library in the system can be sent here. The staff is incredibly helpful, and the entire catalog can be searched online at the URL above.

University of California at San Francisco Libraries

Parnassus, 530 Parnassus Avenue; (415) 476-2334

Mission Bay Library at the Community Center, 1675 Owens Street, Room 150; (415) 514-4060

www.library.ucsf.edu

It's free for the public to come and peruse the library's extensive holdings of health and medical files, including the special Tobacco Control Archives, but users must pay to check out a book and become an active library member—$40 for six months. Note that books may be limited, but that the reference collections of medical texts, periodicals, and journals are extensive. Online search tools are well kept and helpful, and on-site study rooms and computer labs that are available to the public are an added bonus (and cheaper than your local coffee shop when you add up the cost of six months of lattes).

THE CATCH

$40 ($20 for students with ID) for six months' access.

NEWSPAPERS: THE FREE PRESS

Asian Week: www.asianweek.com

Bay Area Reporter (B.A.R.): www.ebar.com

Berkeley Daily Planet: www.berkeleydailyplanet.com

Beyond Chron: www.beyondchron.org

The East Bay Express: www.eastbayexpress.com

El Bohemio (in Spanish): www.bohemionews.com/index.php

The Irish Herald: www.irish-herald.com

J.—The Jewish News Weekly of California: www.jewishsf.com

The San Francisco Bay Guardian: www.sfbg.com

San Francisco Business Times: www.bizjournals.com/sanfrancisco

The San Francisco Examiner: www.examiner.com

San Francisco Sentinel: www.sanfranciscosentinel.com

The San Francisco Weekly: www.sfweekly.com

The Wave: www.thewavemedia.com

The Woofer Times: www.woofertimes.com

Neighborhood Papers

Nob Hill Gazette: www.nobhillgazette.com

The Noe Valley Voice: www.noevalleyvoice.com

Richmond ReView: www.sunsetbeacon.com

San Francisco Bay View: www.sfbayview.com

San Francisco Downtown: www.sfdowntown.com

Sunset Beacon: www.sunsetbeacon.com

Visitacian Valley Grapevine: www.visvalleygrapevine.com

FREE YOUR TV

Free television channels, no cable required.

CBS5: http://cbs5.com

KCSM Public Television: www.kcsm.com

KGO-TV: http://abclocal.go.com/kgo/

KQED Public Television: www.kqed.org

KRON TV 4: www.kron4.com

KTEH Public Television: www.kteh.org

KTSF: www.ktsf.com

KTVU-TV 2: www.ktvu.com

NBC11: www.nbc11.com

{ PETS: }
FREE-ROAMING FINDS

"Money will buy you a fine dog,
but only love can make it
wag its tail."

—*Richard Friedman*

Fido and Fifi deserve the best. However, they're stuck with a cheapskate like you, so second best will have to suffice. While some pampered pets lay atop plush velvet pillows that their owners paid too much for, your little darlings will still know that you love them if they're adorned with a secondhand collar and a comfy bed of used carpet squares. OK, maybe that's too low rent, but that doesn't mean a responsible caregiver can't save a few bucks while trying to give the best to our furry friends. Here are a few tips that will leave you with more leftover cash for kibble.

City of Berkeley Spay Neuter Your Pet (SNYP)

The Berkeley Animal Care Shelter
2013 Second Street, Berkeley
(510) 981-6600
www.ci.berkeley.ca.us/animalservices/SNYPvoucherprog.html

Because the city values pet control over profits, any pet owner in the city of Berkeley may have his or her animal fixed—just $25 for dogs and $15 for cats. Participants must call a participating veterinarian for a voucher and then bring their animal to the shelter for the surgery. Prearrangements are necessary.

The East Bay Society for the Prevention of Cruelty to Animals
8323 Baldwin Street, Oakland; (510) 569-1606

410 Hegenberger Loop, Oakland; (510) 639-7387

www.eastbayspca.org

Keep your eyes on the Web site, as this organization has a lot to offer the cash-poor pet-loving community. There's a regular pet loss support group as well as free classes in pet first aid. A handful of days a year, they offer the very popular free shot days, where anyone can come for canine and feline vaccinations and microchips at whatever donation they can afford (or not). The organization donates crates and flat collars (rather than chains) as needed. The regular pet services in the veterinary clinic are stupendous, available to all pets and owners, and dirt cheap—with visits starting at just $30 and vaccines at $15 each.

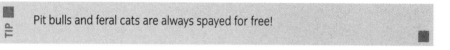

TIP — Pit bulls and feral cats are always spayed for free!

Friends of San Francisco Animal Care and Control
1200 15th Street
(415) 822-5566
www.FSFACC.org

In the unlikely event that your cat or dog strays from home, the new and flawless tracking solution is microchipping, the collar tag of the modern age. Many owners pay up to $80 for this tiny and, they say, safe device to be inserted under the pet's skin, but on several special days throughout the year, this nonprofit, volunteer-run organization gives it away for free to SF residents. If you don't live in the city, the service is just $15.

THE CATCH — A minimum $10 donation is requested, but it is not necessary for service.

Fix Our Ferals
(510) 433-9446
www.fixourferals.org

Granted, feral animals aren't exactly pets, but they can become pets perhaps, and arguably their well-being means that your pet kitty is better protected from disease and other hazards of overpopulation. Thus, this nonprofit organization serving Alameda and Contra Costa Counties will spay or neuter any wild, trapped cat that you bring in. They'll give feline vaccines and any sort of necessary medical treatment, such as for minor wounds and parasites. They'll even allow you to borrow traps to get the cats in for treatments.

THE CATCH — Reservations are a must. Full instructions for animal care are a bit complicated; it's best to read them all on the Web site. They will not treat any animal with a collar.

PET PERSONALS

Not everyone is as responsible as you are, and people part with their animals all the time. Their loss, however, could mean your gain. Whether you like 'em tall and lean or short and chunky, your ideal furry or feathered friend awaits. But however shall you meet? These local and national resources are your best bets for the perfect pet:

- *Craigslist.org has a pets section, but buyers should beware of truly finding a "purebred" anything.*

- *Petfinder.org is an extremely thorough national resource that allows pet seekers to find their soul mate with a succinct list of search criteria. Browsers can hunt based on species, breed, age, and zip code, just to name a few, and peruse adoptable pets from numerous local rescue groups all at once.*

Petco

1685 Bryant Street; (415) 863-1840

1591 Sloat Boulevard; (415) 665-3700

2552 Taylor Street; (415) 440-0423

www.luvmypet.com

National low-cost vaccine company Luv My Pet sets up shop in pet stores in twenty-three states across the country and offers packages of vaccines for dogs, cats, puppies, and kittens for less than most veterinarians—usually around $50 to $60 for several shots. They have locations throughout the Bay Area, but the above locations feature the low-cost vaccines most Saturdays or Sundays. The schedule sometimes changes, so contact the location nearest you.

Pet Food Express

1975 Market Street; (415) 431-4567

3160 Twentieth Avenue; (415) 759-7777

1101 University Avenue, Berkeley; (510) 540-7777

5144 Broadway, Oakland; (510) 654-8888

6398 Telegraph Avenue, Oakland; (510) 923-9500

www.happypet.com

This monster retailer features low-priced weekend vet care at all of its Northern California locations; a regular regimen of vaccines for cats or dogs costs around $40. In addition, this retailer offers microchipping, blood and fecal testing, flea and tick control, ear mite treatment, deworming, and heartworm prevention through a traveling, mobile clinic. Though nothing can replace the attentive care of regular vet visits, this is a good way to save a few bucks and shop for kibble and squeaky balls at the same time.

San Francisco Society for the Prevention of Cruelty to Animals

2500 16th Street
(415) 554-3000
www.sfspca.org

The main draw here is the Spay and Neuter Clinic, which performs the service on your dog or cat for around $100—cheaper than most private vets. Additionally, the SFSPCA offers low-cost health-care services for pets of seniors and the homeless, plus no-interest loans for pets that require emergency services. If you're seeking pet-friendly housing, they keep a list of landlords who will allow you and your four paws on premises, available gratis. And in the terrible and unlikely event that you'll ever need it, they also offer a free weekly pet loss support group for affected families.

{ **SECTION 3:**
EXPLORING
SAN FRANCISCO }

{ TRANSPORTATION: }
THE ONLY WAY TO FLY

"Who is rich? He that is content.
Who is that? Nobody."

–Benjamin Franklin

Planes, trains, and wheels—San Francisco's 7 by 7 miles of terrain aren't much to traverse geographically, but when every nook and cranny are packed with so much to see and do, you'll want to cover as much of it as you can—and get around as freely, and with as much freedom, as possible. The city is well served by the MUNI bus system (though there are plenty of exceptions to this rule, depending on location, time of day, and all-too-frequent breakdowns), but it's not uncommon for the wait for the bus and the bus ride itself to take the same amount of time as walking. With a little insider know-how, forethought, and a bit of luck, one can see this town hobo-style—totally free, or for cheaper than the average price.

PUBLIC TRANSPORTATION

Bay Area Rapid Transit (BART)
www.bart.gov/tickets/types/types.asp
BART does not offer weekly or monthly passes for regular East Bay–bound commuters unless you are a school-age student, disabled, or over age sixty-five. Those who take BART within the city may benefit from the purchase of a half-monthly BART Plus Ticket, which allows for transport on MUNI and the San Francisco BART stations and many other Bay Area transportation systems.

Blue and Gold Fleet
www.blueandgoldfleet.com
Though mainly a tour operator on the water and on land, this company also offers a small amount of commuter ferries, like those between San Francisco and Sausalito and Tiburon to the north. Web-only specials run periodically that allow for the purchase of twenty regular adult tickets for just $100–a substantial savings of $70.00 off purchasing individual adult tickets at the $8.50 retail price.

THE CATCH

These tickets are only good Monday through Friday, catering to a mostly commuter audience. If you're visiting the area or if you have tourists in town to entertain, check out the periodic Internet specials.

Caltrain

www.caltrain.com/schedule_tickets.html

Travelers commuting mainly to the South Bay can buy a monthly pass and a ten-ride pass, but it's unlikely they'll save much money unless they take more than ten rides per week. However, those connecting with the Santa Clara Valley Transport Authority or SamTrans with a two-zone ticket can transfer onto a bus on either system for free. Regular San Francisco MUNI riders can add a MUNI sticker to their monthly Caltrain pass for just $40—which is $5 off the price of a regular MUNI Fast Pass alone.

Golden Gate Ferry

http://goldengateferry.org/fareprograms/cashfares.php

Both a bus system and a ferry serving Marin County to the north and its onslaught of commuters who come into SF every day, the ferry offers discount programs to save the working person a few dollars as he or she crosses counties. Ride Value Discount Ticket Books offer 20 percent off the regular price of a one-way adult ferry ticket for boats that run between SF's Ferry Building and Marin's Larkspur and Sausalito. Books must be purchased in packs of twenty. Half-off tickets are also available for youths under age seventeen, those over sixty-five, and people with disabilities.

THE CATCH
Discount ticket books expire in six months. Use 'em or lose 'em.

TIP
This is one of the most economical ways in the area to get your landlubbing self a thirty- to forty-five-minute ride on the beautiful bay.

San Francisco Municipal Railway (MUNI)

www.sfmuni.com

Love it, hate it—no matter how you feel about it, everyone rides San Francisco's favorite (and only) bus and light-rail system. Though its quality and reliability ebbs and flows, the price keeps going up and up—but luckily there are ways to save a few dollars while getting around town. Regular riders will benefit from a weekly pass for just $15 (at a buck and a half a ride, this breaks basic commuters even). Better yet, buy the Fast Pass for $45 before the first of the month to take full advantage of free rides on both MUNI and BART and SamTrans (in SF only). Discounts are also available for youth, the elderly, and the disabled. Purchasing locations are listed on the Web site.

TIP
Always take a transfer. When boarding a bus on street level, it pays to flash today's transfer casually to the driver—even if the time has expired. More often than not, you can get the ride for free. Don't bother trying this tactic riding the lettered trains that board underground. For some reason, these MUNI operators take their job very seriously, and it's likely they won't let you through the gate. Note that this isn't official policy, so you didn't hear this trick from us. . . .

SAVE MONEY AND TIME WITH FASTRAK

www.bayareafastrak.org

Owning a car is expensive in San Francisco, no matter how you slice it. Yet there are a couple of ways to save a few bucks when it comes to coughing up for bridge toll. With the handy FasTrak pass, one can traverse the Golden Gate Bridge for a buck less (just $4), though shuffling east on the Bay Bridge remains the same price as those who don't have the windshield-affixed tag ($3). Hybrid drivers and those vehicles with three passengers or more during rush hour get passage totally free. The best part? No more scrounging for change and dollars in the ashtray..

TO AND FROM THE AIRPORT

San Francisco International (SFO)

TIP
For free information about your transportation options in and out of the airport, dial *1121 from any courtesy phone on premises at the airport, or 511 from any regular telephone.

Public Transportation

BART

The train now goes directly into SFO's domestic terminal, and this is certainly your cheapest route to meet your plane—short of begging a new lover to drive you down. This train connects with all of BART's usual stations throughout San Francisco and the East Bay. Costs vary depending on the length of your trip, but one-way from SF's Mission and 16th Streets station is just $5.10. To view a schedule and calculate the cost of your trip, visit www.bart.gov or call (650) 992-2278. Note that the BART train also connects passengers with the Caltrain system at Milbrae, serving the South Bay, including Palo Alto and Gilroy.

SamTrans

This also connects the airport with the public transportation system of San Mateo twenty-four hours a day, including routes KX, 292, and 397. Routes 292 and 397 also stop at SFO's Rental Car Center and the United Airlines Maintenance Center. For more information visit www.samtrans.com or call (800) 660-4287.

Door-to-Door Vans Serving SFO

Particularly for passengers traveling alone with too much luggage to carry on their own, this is the next most affordable option in and out of the airport. Prices hover around $20 per passenger one-way. To find these vans at SFO, simply go up one level from Baggage Claim and follow the signs for door-to-door transportation. Expect most of these shysters to try to pack the van for the maximum number of riders; it's not uncommon for the driver to make four or five stops at various locations all over the city, particularly on your way home.

THE CATCH: Reservations are necessary to get you to the airport, but not necessary upon leaving SFO.

Advanced Airport Shuttle, (650) 504-6641

Airport Express, (415) 775-5121

American Airporter Shuttle, (415) 202-0733, (800) 282-7758

Bay Shuttle, (415) 564-3400

Lorrie's Airport Shuttle, (415) 334-9000

M & M Luxury Shuttle, (415) 552-3200

Pacific Airport Shuttle, (415) 681-6318

Peter's Airport Shuttle, (650) 577-8858

Quake City Shuttle, (415) 255-4899, (415) 621-2831

San Francisco City Shuttle, (888) 850-7878

SuperShuttle, (415) 558-8500

Taxis

Follow the signs out of Baggage Claim toward the taxi stand. Taxis in and out of SFO run around $40 to $50 one-way, and passengers pay the metered fare. Oddly enough, for two or more passengers, this is not much more expensive than paying for a door-to-door shuttle van service (such as Super Shuttle, M & M, and Quake City, most of which usually cost around $15 to $20 per person, plus tip), and a cab will get you there a whole lot quicker. If you are a lone traveler leaving the airport during regular hours and you'd like to split the cost of the trip with a stranger, it pays to walk up to the line and ask if anyone is heading in your same direction. If you're both going toward adjacent neighborhoods in SF and you both have cash, it's a good idea to share the cost of the ride.

Oakland International Airport

Public Transportation

AC Transit

For the price of regular bus fair (around $2), East Bay residents can ride directly to the airport on bus lines 50 and N. The N line also runs directly into SF's downtown Transbay Terminal, though the route is pretty slow. Some hours are limited, and some additional fares may apply. Learn more at www.actransit.org or (800) 448-9790.

BART/AirBART

Every ten to twenty minutes all day, except for late at night, BART riders can transfer at the Coliseum Station to catch the AirBART, which will take them directly to the airport for $2 on top of the price of the regular BART fare. For more information go to www.bart.gov or call (510) 465-BART.

Door-to-Door Shuttle Services Serving SF and the East Bay

Since Oakland is a smaller airport, it costs more to get there, despite the fact that it's not much farther away. Expect to pay about $35 per person, one-way, to ride one of these shuttle services.

A-1 Express Shuttle Service, (888) 676-0565

Acropolis Airport Shuttle, (510) 827-5894

Air-Transit Shuttle, (510) 568-3434

American Airport Shuttle, (415) 202-0733

American Shuttle Express, (408) 259-9500

Angel Express, (866) 295-3797

Apollo Shuttle, (925) 755-8892

Avon Airporter Express, (888) 592-2866

B.A.B.E.S. Airporter, (510) 317-6983

Bay Airporter Express, (510) 234-9759

Bay Area Shuttle, (510) 324-3000

Bay Shuttle, (415) 564-3400

Bay Transit Shuttle, (510) 714-4000

Bayporter Express, (415) 467-1800

Best Way Shuttle, (925) 363-7711

Bridge Airporter, (510) 867-1476

City Express Shuttle, (888) 874-8885

Citywide Shuttle, (510) 816-8569

E-Z Ride Airporter, (510) 393-5554

Flying Eagle Shuttle, (510) 259-0095

Horizon Airporter, (510) 333-4778

Lucky Shuttle, (510) 303-8772

Luxor Shuttle, (510) 562-7222

Quake City Shuttle Inc., (415) 255-4899

Safety Express Shuttle, (510) 388-2029

Shuttle Pro, (866) 499-2447

Silicon Valley Airporter, (650) 869-4476

Silverline Airporter, (510) 259-8609

Super Shuttle, (800) 258-3826

Take Me Home Express, (510) 652-8700

Traveler Shuttle, (510) 909-0965

Tri City Airport Shuttle, (510) 812-3324

USA Shuttle, (510) 744-0222

US Airporter, (510) 223-1228

Taxis

A private car to and from Oakland airport runs around $60 to $65 between the airport and SF. Since the crowd tends to be smaller, sharing one with a stranger is a trickier task.

BICYCLES

It's a means of transportation, it's a vehicle for social change. Whether you bike around town for recreation or rely on two wheels for your daily commute, these places can help make your ride smoother.

Bike Hut at South Beach

Pier 40 (Embarcadero and Townsend)
(415) 543-4335
www.thebikehut.com

Here bicycles in the South of Market area can be rented, repaired, and sold while bringing needed funds and social skills to the stratas of the population who need it most, as this shop works with local nonprofit and job skills organizations. Bikes rent for as little as $5 an hour and are sold for as little as $40. Check them out for some of the best-priced deals on two wheels.

Craigslist

http://sfbay.craigslist.org/bik/

How many times can we list this bulletin board as a resource? Only when it really is the shopper's best bet for cheap stuff. And if you're looking for a cool bike that's not too "hot," if you know what we mean, this is one of the most affordable bike "shops" in town. Buyer beware, but you can ride away with a great bargain on two wheels.

The Missing Link Bicycle Cooperative

1988 Shattuck Avenue, Berkeley
(510) 843-7471
www.missinglink.org

For thirty years this twenty-or-so member co-op has been keeping the pedal-friendly East Bay moving through a collaboration of low-cost bikes for sale and a community outreach program that offers free loaner tools to do your own bike repair. The free classes will teach you how to do it. There's also a fairly priced repair shop, used bikes for purchase, a calendar of community rides, and more.

PLAN IT MORE, PEDAL LESS

Bicycling.511.org

If you're trying to build the kind of thigh muscles that turn heads, then feel free to ride San Francisco's endless, steep hills to your heart's content. But if you'd just like to commute around town as safely, effortlessly, and as stress free as possible, take advantage of this free, online collection of interactive bicycling maps and bike route planners. Your quads will thank you.

Pedal Revolution

3085 21st Street
(415) 641-1264
www.pedalrevolution.com

Yes, it's retail, but it's also a nonprofit organization and oh so much more. In addition to selling new bikes, Pedal offers a great selection of secondhand and refurbished models at fair prices, new and used parts, and professional bike repair. This organization provides employment opportunities and teaches real-world career skills to kids ages fourteen to twenty-one interested in bicycling and bike repair.

TIP

For $30 a year, those who want to fix their own bikes, but lack the tools and space to do it, can schedule access to Pedal's many workbenches and use their tools while hitting up staff for assistance (when available). Periodically they offer free workshops for members and nonmembers that will teach you to fix your bike yourself. Beat that, cheapskate!

San Francisco Bike Kitchen

1256 Mission Street (entrance on Laskie)
www.bikekitchen.org

Even cheaper than Pedal Revolution, this DIY repair shop provides the space and resources to let you fix your own two-wheeled steed for just $5 a day or $30 per year. But even if you can't afford the fee for services, a few hours of volunteering will buy you the same access in trade. Deep lovers of bicycling can volunteer to start earning a bike frame and parts to build their own rig. Inquire about their house Earn-a-Bike program for those with lots of time and enthusiasm but short on cash. Fee-based classes are offered on premises that teach the basics of bike building and bike repair.

{PUBLIC ART} AND ATTRACTIONS:
SHOW ME THE MONET

"If wealth is found by rejecting the experience of poverty, then it will never be complete. The soul is nurtured by want as much as by plenty."

—*Thomas Moore*

Beauty is in the eye of the beholder, and when beauty is being given away, it truly is a sight to behold. San Francisco is a stunning city with loads of vistas that are easy on the eyes. But when the cranial sensibilities crave a bit of manmade sophistication, the city's bustling arts scene is a bounty of entertainment. From fast street art to the slicked-up MoMA, from the careful cultivation of a well-sculpted garden to the plethora of galleries and museums that dot the neighborhoods, the well-planned lover of aesthetics will feast. Visitors and locals alike cannot overlook the streamlined eye candy of some of San Francisco's sauciest and best-known landmarks, such as the Dr. Seuss-y twist of Lombard Street or the colorful swath of the Golden Gate Bridge. They are proof that art is everywhere, and that creative expression courses through our metropolitan veins.

WALKING TOURS

Strap on your fancy footwear and pack the binoculars. We've got a city to conquer.

Barbary Coast Trail
www.sfhistory.org

The San Francisco Museum and Historical Society has put together this interesting, free, 4-mile self-guided walking tour ripe with city history. It covers twenty historical sites of interest, stunning views, and beautiful main streets and side alleys in a handful of diverse neighborhoods. While whole books are available that detail the finer points of every stop, bare-bones information and a printable map are available on the Web site above for the public to download at will.

City Guides Walking Tours

www.sfcityguides.org

From brothels to hotels, from whole neighborhoods to San Francisco's forests and murals, this outstanding resource offers a busy calendar of free ways to access the history and lore of our fair city on your own two feet, and it's a popular pastime for visitors and local residents alike. Volunteer tour leaders are a font of knowledge on their particular subject matter as well as city history, and many of them share firsthand and personal knowledge and experience as well.

THE CATCH } This is sponsored by the public library, but a donation envelope is passed at the end with a request for funds to keep the program going. Cash is requested but not required.

On The Level SF

www.onthelevelsf.com

Let's face it—San Francisco is a topographical destination, but one that's not easily navigable by everyone. Sometimes shorter, accessible walking tours (without hills!) are a necessity even for folks who have walking stamina. People with some limited mobility will rejoice to find this collection of free, self-guided walking tours that explore some of the area's most interesting neighborhoods. While this company does offer some services that cost money—such as guided tours or tours that involve meals—anyone can go to the Web site and download the information on self-guided tours to destinations like Golden Gate Park and the Marina Green.

San Francisco Botanical Garden at Strybing Arboretum

Ninth Avenue (at Lincoln Way), Golden Gate Park

(415) 661-1316, ext. 312

www.sfbotanicalgarden.org

Trained and knowledgeable garden-loving docents offer daily, totally free tours of this exemplary botanical garden. Anyone with a green thumb should snatch up this opportunity. Those who prefer to trod the green path solo can download a walking map from the Web site or pick up a self-guided brochure on-site.

San Francisco City Hall Tours

1 Dr. Carlton B. Goodlett Place, Room 008

Office of the Building General Manager

(415) 554-4933

www.sfgov.org

Monday through Friday, 10:00 a.m., noon, and 2:00 p.m.

The massive, golden rotunda in San Francisco's Civic Center is truly a sight to behold, and those interested in this architectural masterpiece of Arthur Brown Jr. and John Bakewell Jr. will enjoy these daily, free, guided tours of one of city government's most interesting and talked-about buildings. Visitors must sign up for tours at the information/tour kiosk near the front door. Private tours can be arranged for large groups.

San Francisco Parks Trust Park Guides

(415) 263-0991

www.sfpt.org

From city statues to the historic Japanese Tea Garden, from stroller walks to the AIDS Grove—locals and visitors should not squander this free opportunity to get to know one of the city's largest parks more intimately. Educated guides will take you windmill to windmill or lake to lake, and best of all, it's unlikely they will get you lost—quite a feat among the park's numerous twisty paths and turns. These tours are your city's tax dollars at work for something great.

MURALS

An empty wall is just a white canvas for San Francisco's many artists. We're not talking about graffiti here: These murals are requested, planned, and exquisitely executed. On a sunny day a mural tour is one of the best ways to view the entire city as a gallery.

Balmy Alley and 24th Street

In the heart of the Latino-rich Mission District, this brilliant depiction of political struggle and Latin American cultural heroes makes a bold statement on a questionable block.

Beach Chalet

1000 Great Highway

(415) 386-8439

http://beachchalet.com

It took two years to paint, but the glorious and colorful depictions inside this historic building at the edge of Golden Gate Park and Ocean Beach were well worth the effort. Artist Lucien Labaudt toiled tirelessly to capture the images and sensations of San Francisco during the Great Depression, and he captured every corner of the city in the process, from Fisherman's Wharf to South of Market. Also on display in the lobby: more historic memorabilia and an excellent model of Golden Gate Park. While you're here, pop into the restaurant upstairs for a cocktail and a great ocean view.

Clarion Alley and Valencia Street

This alley may not smell so fresh, but its visual allure and fresco designs make it a must-see for fans of folk art and hip-hop alike. Rather than one simple statement, several artists share this long public street, thus the experience is diverse and ever changing. Keep your eyes on the walls for the date of the annual block party, when residents come out to celebrate the latest installations and revel in the overall hipness.

Coit Tower

1 Telegraph Hill
(415) 362-0808

At the bequest of SF socialite and philanthropist Lillie Coit, this popular landmark features spectacular views of the Bay Area on the outside and unforgettable World War II–era political murals inside its large rotunda. Every so often the city considers charging tourists an entrance fee to pay for its preservation, but for now stepping in to view the ground floor is free.

Duboce Bikeway Mural

Duboce and Church Streets
www.monacaron.com/murals.html

Mona Caron, the celebrated artist behind the Market Street Railway mural, made her name with this transcendent and dreamy bike-ride depiction of Northern California's best outdoor scenery. Never before has the back of a Safeway supermarket looked so good. MUNI riders are spared what would have undoubtedly been a frequently graffittied concrete wall; instead they ride off into the sunset. Those pressed for time can simply take the J Church or the N Judah past for a quick view, but there's so much detail that the mural is best savored by foot.

MaestraPeace at the Women's Building

3543 18th Street
(415) 431-1180
www.womensbuilding.org

Finished in 1994, this massive building on a whole square block bursts with color that's a multiethnic, multigenerational celebration of women through the ages. A team of seven women artists joined forces to memorialize female icons and their accomplishments from around the globe.

The Making of a Fresco [Making a Fresco] Showing the Building of a City
At the Art Institute of San Francisco
800 Chestnut Street
(415) 771-7020
www.sanfranciscoart.edu

Famed artist and muralist Diego Rivera crafted this metamural, highlighting the creation of a fresco within a fresco, in 1931. Those who worked with him on the piece are immortalized here. This is one of Rivera's four murals that made their mark on the city. It is the magnet drawing people to the student art gallery, which is open free to the general public.

Market Street Railway Mural
Church and 15th Streets
www.monacaron.com/murals.html

This award-winning newcomer among San Francisco's most notable murals is a multipaneled elapsed time capsule of Market Street through the decades. Painted on a convenience-store wall, cable cars, automobiles, and pedestrians share visual space on this portrayal of the historic thoroughfare. It's worthy of more than a casual second glance.

Marriage of the Artistic Expression of the North and of the South on this Continent
(commonly known as *Pan American Unity*)
At City College of San Francisco
50 Phelan Avenue
(415) 239-3000
www.riveramural.org

Mexican goddesses and Indian woodcarvers are the crux of this piece, perhaps SF's most famous mural, painted by Diego Rivera in 1940. This must-see contribution proudly adorns the Diego Rivera Theater, and surely it has inspired more than one student to reach a higher level of excellence. The main theme of the piece is to create a unified America, bringing the continent's central and southern residents into the northern fold.

CEMETERIES/CREMATORIUMS

The Cemetery at Mission Dolores Basilica
3321 16th Street
(415) 621-8203
www.missiondolores.org

Although this beautiful and historic mission is the final resting place of more than 5,000 American Indians, this ancient cemetery, dating from 1830, commemorates some of San Francisco's most famous names that now adorn street signs, such as Arguello, Frederick, Balboa, and more. These ancient stone markers and their surrounding gardens are truly a sight to behold. While you're here, be sure to tour the historic mission itself, once visited by the Pope and home to generations of worshippers.

Chapel of the Chimes
4499 Piedmont Avenue, Oakland
(510) 654-0123
www.chapelofthechimes.com

It's a crematorium, plus a whole lot more! Visitors will be absolutely enthralled by the Julia Morgan building's unforgettable architecture and design. But there's plenty to do here for the living as well. The site houses regular coffee club gatherings, author readings, and our favorite—Jazz at the Chimes, which is ten bucks well spent for a weekend afternoon so entertaining that people are just dying to get in.

Pet Cemetery at the Presidio
Northwestern corner of San Francisco
(415) 561-4323 (information)
www.nps.gov/prsf

No one seems to know how it started, but an ancient, well-maintained pet burial ground on a military base is absolutely a site worthy of a visit. Here the rodents, dogs, cats, and birds of colonels, generals, and other high-ranking military personnel come to rest, with proper epitaphs and headstones to boot. As in any other sacred final resting place, the intrepid can find several unknown markers—as no one should forget the guinea pig that died in honor of his country.

The San Francisco Columbarium
1 Loraine Court
(415) 752-7891

Tucked into SF's Outer Richmond district, this crematorium has about 7,500 "apartments" in which the deceased can rest, but it likely houses the remains of 65,000 inhabitants. Now run by the Neptune Society, the beautiful Victorian building is more than a hundred years old and features three stories of ancient burial vaults.

The San Francisco National Cemetery
At the Presidio, northwestern corner of SF
(415) 561-4323 (information)
www.nps.gov/prsf

More than 30,000 soldiers have been laid to rest here among the twenty-eight acres in the Old Presidio Army Base. The site is part of the National Park Service and the Golden Gate National Recreation Area. The look of the headstones has the understatement of an Arlington National, but the first honorees to be interned here date from 1854. This is the largest remaining cemetery in San Francisco.

PUBLIC GARDENS

Conservatory of Flowers
JFK Drive, Golden Gate Park
(415) 666-7001
www.conservatoryofflowers.org

If you just haven't the time to jet down to Bali or Brazil for a traipse through an enchanted rain forest, this stunning plant collection, viewable on the cheap, is the next best alternative. The rare collection of orchids, bromeliads, and other tropical species from around the globe are breathtaking, and even more so for the green thumb among us. The building itself is not to be missed: The oldest conservatory in the Western Hemisphere dates from 1878 and reopened its doors in 2003 after a vigorous restoration.

THE CATCH

Admission is $5; free entry the first Tuesday of the month.

TIP

In summer the popping hues of the nearby Dahlia Garden, to the right of the conservatory when facing its front doors, absolutely should not be missed.

Japanese Tea Garden
Off JFK Drive, Golden Gate Park
(415) 752-4227

It's listed in every tourist guidebook and for good reason: This easy, sculpted stroll through carefully shaped trees, well-appointed stones and bridges, and clear, koi-stocked ponds instantly puts the mind at ease. Since 1894 this has been a showcase for Japanese and Chinese native flora, and it's worth a visit anytime—though in summer the tourist foot traffic can make the garden feel as crowded as a Tokyo subway. The shaded teahouse on premises may not be the most authentic, but it's still a lovely place to take a date or whittle away a warm afternoon for just a few dollars.

THE CATCH

Garden admission is $4; free entry Monday, Wednesday, and Friday, 9:00 to 10:00 A.M.

San Francisco Botanical Garden at Strybing Arboretum

Ninth Avenue at Lincoln Way, Golden Gate Park

(415) 564-3239

www.sfbotanicalgarden.org

This breathtaking urban oasis of natural beauty features plant species from all over the world, plus a library and free guided walking tours every single day of the year. This fenced-in resource is a pristine, dog-free must-see in one of SF's largest and most populated parks—and a great place to feed the waterfowl to boot.

Yerba Buena Gardens

Between 3rd and 4th Streets on Mission Street

OK, essentially this is just a park. But what makes this spot of green worthy of a mention is its location. This is one of the few places where your butt can touch grass in the Downtown area (though technically it's SoMa, but not by much). There's a wonderful fountain to walk beneath and get inspired by quotes from Martin Luther King Jr. Short of a spa break on your lunch hour, this is the next best way to rejuvenate and get away from your crappy temp job's bland four walls.

WHAT'S THE DIFFERENCE BETWEEN LARKSPUR AND CALLA LILIES?

Find out by procuring the annual free gardening calendar from the San Francisco Public Utilities Commission Water Pollution Prevention Program. Every September San Francisco residents are welcome to log on to the utility's Web site and request the free gardening calendar for the following year, which features brilliant photography, events of interest to those who love to tend the earth, and tips on less-toxic gardening. It's available online only at http://sfwater.org/mto_main.cfm/MC_ID/17/ MSC_ID/197/MTO_ID/388. Or visit www.sfwater.org, and click on "Education," then "Tips for the Garden."

Community Gardens

Community Gardens Program

Sponsored by San Francisco Recreation and Parks

(415) 581-2541 (information)

http://parks.sfgov.org/site/recpark_index.asp?id=27048

San Francisco has more than forty small plots of volunteer-run, first come, first served community gardens that are free for public use (though most gardens pool together small sums to cover common expenses). These are lovely to visit, particularly during the growing season, and they're even more fun to cultivate. Look for signs posted around the gardens in your community, as many neighborhoods use these spaces for social gatherings, holiday sales, and more.

Bayview/Hunter's Point: Adam Rogers Park, Ingalls at Oakdale

Bernal Heights: Gates at Banks; Prospect at Courtland; Ogden Terraces, Ogden and Prentiss; Park Street, Park and San Jose

Corona Heights: States at Museum; Crags Court, Crags at Berkeley

Crocker Amazon: Moscow at Geneva; Dublin at Russia

Dogpatch: Brewster at Rutledge

Eureka Valley: Corwin at Douglass

Glen Park: Arlington at Highland

The Haight: Koshland Park Community Learning Garden, Page at Buchanan; Page and Laguna Mini Park

Mission District: Alioto Mini Park, 20th Street at Capp; KidPower Park, 45 Hoff Street at 16th Street; Treat Commons at Parque Ninos Unidos, 23rd Street and Treat; Potrero del Sol, Cesar Chavez and Potrero

Nob Hill: Mason at Pine

Noe Valley: Clipper and Grandview

North Beach: Michelangelo Playground, Greenwich at Jones

Outer Mission: Lessing/Sears Mini Park

Potrero Hill: 25th Street at De Haro; 22nd Street and Arkansas; 22nd Street and Connecticut; 20th Street and San Bruno Avenue

Richmond District: Golden Gate Senior Center; 37th Street at Fulton

South of Market: Howard/Langton Mini Park; Folsom and Sherman

St. Mary's Park: Alemany at Ellsworth

Sunset District: White Crane Springs; South of Seventh Avenue and Lawton

Upper Market: Noe/Beaver Mini Park

Visitacion Valley: McLaren Park, Leland at Hahn; Visitacion Valley Greenway, Arleta at Rutland

ART GALLERIES

First Thursdays Downtown

Mark your calendars now. On the first Thursday of every month, almost all of the posh Downtown galleries in SF open up their doors after hours to the after-work crowd, and this means free art spying, free scene schmoozing, and lotsa, lotsa free wine and cheese. Most of the galleries are in or around Geary, Post, and Sutter Streets, but all are within a mile of one another on flat, easily walkable streets. You can start anywhere—most stay open until 7:30 p.m. or later—but beginning at the multigalleried 49 Geary space near Market will get you off to a nice start. Nibblers and imbibers can enjoy viewing numerous masters, such as Renoir, Warhol, and Picasso, and many contemporary, lesser known and local talents as well.

All of these galleries are quite accomplished, but here are a few that are sure to entertain:

Graystone, 77 Geary Street; (415) 956-7693

Hang, 556 Sutter Street; (415) 434-4264

Martin Lawrence, 366 Geary Street; (415) 956-0345

Weinstein, 383 Geary Street; (415) 362-8151

Mission Galleries

On the opposite end of the spectrum from Downtown, the lovably downscale Mission District is home to another walkable stretch of great galleries from artists with a flair for a more edgy, raw, or retro aesthetic. Not only are the pieces far more interesting to look at than the polish and sleek that you'll find elsewhere, but the hip scenesters here to admire it are just way, way cooler. If you are an aspiring cheapskate art collector, note that this part of town probably has more pieces than elsewhere that are under $100. And if you have a sharp eye, you may even find pieces being given away for free, stapled to a lamppost or tied to a bicycle rack.

While there are no regular tours or scheduled open houses that bring all of the galleries together, the neighborhood welcomes browsers at all times. For an occasional glass of free Yellow Tail and a cube or two of Trader Joe's Monterey Jack, sign up for each individual gallery's mailing list to be kept informed of openings. Here are a few that always deliver:

Blue Room Gallery, 2331 Mission Street; (415) 282-8411

City Art Gallery, 828 Valencia Street; (415) 970-9900

Creativity Explored, 3245 16th Street; (415) 863-2108

Galeria de la Raza, 2857 24th Street; (415) 826-8009

Jack Hanley Gallery, 395 Valencia Street; (415) 522-1623

66balmy, 66 Balmy Alley; (415) 648-1760

OPEN STUDIOS

Every weekend in October

Think of this as Halloween for art lovers, featuring numerous free treats and very few tricks. Nearly every artist in every neighborhood flings the studio doors wide open and invites the public to come peruse not just the display of finished pieces for sale but also all of the paint-splattered, dust-covered spaces where the works were created. Artworks run the gamut from entirely affordable collage, photorealistic paintings, and expressionistic photography to everything in between. And wherever there are art openings, there's snacking. Wine and chocolates and cheese are as plentiful and as eclectic as the hordes of local arts supporters that parade from door to door.

Do not miss this annual fall visual arts preview. Find the map detailing the hundreds of participating studios in the San Francisco Bay Guardian *or online at www.artspan.org.*

South of Market Galleries

There's a lot of art SoMa, but most of it is mixed with something more, either as part of a multiuse art space or as part of a bar or restaurant. Each visitor will walk away with his or her own impression—is it a bar with some art on the wall, or is it a gallery that just happens to serve drinks? The region encourages visitors to not be such purists about their visual stimulation—that yes, indeed, that mammoth Brian Barneclo painting *does* look better with a DJ soundtrack and a blood orange martini or two. Clearly this is not to everyone's taste. But if you like your sculpture shaken and stirred, come here to imbibe, investigate, and get inspired.

The Luggage Store, 1007 Market Street; (415) 255-5971

111 Minna Gallery, 111 Minna Street; (415) 974-1719

SF Camerawork, 657 Mission Street, Second Floor; (415) 512-2020

Varnish, 77 Natoma Street; (415) 222-6131

Elsewhere in San Francisco

Rx Gallery
132 Eddy Street
(415) 756-8825
www.rxgallery.com

There are parts of town that are more savory than the Tenderloin, but this gallery/lounge is lovely enough to make it worth the trip. Far enough off the beaten path to be underground and known enough to be well attended, the openings here showcase an edgy flavor of emerging talent and are superfun. They are, as is true of almost all openings in the art world, totally free. Sign on to the mailing list to stay informed.

San Francisco Arts Commission Gallery
401 Van Ness Avenue
(415) 554-6080
www.sfacgallery.org

In the Civic Center, among the formal sterility of SF's government buildings, this eye in the storm features a consistent stream of excellent work by local artists. While you're in the area applying for your artistic grant, be sure to stop in for a peek.

San Francisco City Hall
1 Carlton B. Goodlett Place, Room 282
(415) 554-7630
www.sfacgallery.org

Also in the Civic Center, this auxiliary SFAC gallery is another spotlight on local talent, and one that's absolutely worth a visit while you're in applying for your marriage license (gay or straight). These exhibits tend to lean more toward the photographic arts.

San Francisco Recycling and Disposal Artist in Residence Program

503 Tunnel Avenue

(415) 330-1415

www.sfrecyclinganddisposal.com/AIR

Some artists claim that they create from thin air. These thinkers create from garbage. Just a handful of artists are fortunate enough to be allowed residency at the dump—that's right, the trash collector—and as such, they have access to all of the discarded waste and recycling material they could ever dream of. The community is invited to see these raw materials in action at several different art openings a year, and the results are always a remarkable makeover. Come early to sneak a peek at the hefty, waste-crunching machinery on-site and to catch an eyeful of the scavenging birds of prey up above. The smells will be memorable. Stiletto pumps are not advised.

MUSEUMS

Always Free

Cable Car Museum, 1201 Mason Street; (415) 474-1887; www.cablecarmuseum.org.

CCA Wattis Institute for Contemporary Arts, California College of the Arts; 1111 8th Street; www.wattis.org.

Chinese Cultural Center, 750 Kearny Street, Third Floor; (415) 986-1822; www.c-c-c.org.

GLBT Historical Society, 657 Mission Street, #300; (415) 777-5455; www.glbthistory.org.

Museo Italo Americano, Fort Mason Center, Building C; (415) 673-2200; www.museoitaloamericano.org.

Octagon House, 2645 Gough Street; (415) 441-7512. Contributions are welcome, and hours are quite limited. It's best to call before planning a visit.

Randall Museum, 199 Museum Way; (415) 554-9600; www.randallmuseum.org.

San Francisco Fire Department Museum, 655 Presidio Avenue; (415) 563-4630; www.sffiremuseum.org. Hours are limited; best to call ahead.

Often Free

Asian Art Museum, 200 Larkin Street; (415) 581-3500; www.asianart.org. Free the first Tuesday of the month. On Thursday after 5:00 p.m., admission is just $5.

Bay Area Discovery Museum, East Fort Baker, 557 McReynolds Road, Sausalito; (415) 339-3900; www.baykidsmuseum.org. Free the second Saturday of the month after 1:00 p.m. This is great for kids; worth a drive across the bridge.

California Academy of Sciences (Steinhart Aquarium), 875 Howard Street; (415) 321-8000; www.calacademy.org. Free the first Wednesday of the month.

Cartoon Art Museum, 655 Mission Street; (415) 227-8666; www.cartoonart.org. The first Tuesday of the month is "pay what you wish" day.

Chinese Historical Society of America Museum and Learning Center, 965 Clay Street; (415) 391-1188; www.chsa.org. Free the first Thursday of the month.

Contemporary Jewish Museum, 121 Steuart Street; (415) 344-8800; www.jmsf.org. Free the third Monday of the month.

de Young Museum, 50 Hagiwara Tea Garden Drive, Golden Gate Park; (415) 863-3330; www.thinker.org. Free the first Tuesday of the month. On Friday after 5:00 p.m., admission is just $5. Do not miss the view from the top of the tower.

Exploratorium, 3601 Lyon Street; (415) 561-0360; www.exploratorium.edu. Free the first Wednesday of the month.

Legion of Honor, Thirty-fourth Avenue at Clement Street, Lincoln Park; (415) 863-3330; www.thinker.org. Free the first Tuesday of the month. MUNI riders with a Fast Pass or transfer always receive $2 off regular admission.

Musee Mecanique, Pier 45, Shed A; (415) 346-2000; www.museemechanique.org. There is no admission fee, but all of the attractions are coin operated. For the truly penny-pinching, enjoyment can be had by enjoying the turn-of-the-twentieth-century amusements on someone else's quarter. This is especially true of the collection's many player pianos.

Museum of Craft and Folk Art, 51 Yerba Buena Lane; www.mocfa.org. Free the first Tuesday of the month.

The Mexican Museum, Fort Mason Center Building D, Marina Boulevard at Buchanan Street; (415) 202-9700; www.mexicanmuseum.org. Free the first Wednesday of the month. Note that at press time, the museum was temporarily closed for a move into Yerba Buena. Check the Web site for more details.

San Francisco Museum of Craft & Design, 550 Sutter Street; (415) 773-0303; www.sfmcd.org. Free every first Thursday after 5:00 p.m.

San Francisco Museum of Modern Art, 151 3rd Street; (415) 357-4000; www.sfmoma.org. Free the first Tuesday of the month, and admission is half price on Thursday after 6:00 p.m.

San Francisco Zoo, Sloat Boulevard at Great Highway; (415) 753-7080; www.sfzoo.org. Free the first Wednesday of the month, with discounts every day for SF residents with proof of residence.

Yerba Buena Center for the Arts, 701 Mission Street; (415) 978-2700; www.ybca.org. Free the first Tuesday of the month

SO VERY SF

Elevator of the Hyatt Regency Embarcadero Hotel

5 Embarcadero Center
(415) 433-3717

The foot of Market Street is home to one of the area's best glass elevators. It soars seventeen stories through the mammoth, retro-era atrium. Walk in like you own the place and take 'em for a spin—you'll be surprised how much it feels like a roller coaster.

The Golden Gate Bridge

Most folks drive the bridge during their daily commute and forget to notice its beauty, but those who savor life's free bounty should walk this splendid city land-mark. Enjoy panoramic bay views of Angel Island, Alcatraz, teams of sailboats, and the statuesque presence of the bridge itself.

The Grace Cathedral Labyrinth

1100 California Street
(415) 749-6300
www.gracecathedral.org

Quiet your mind and take a walk within the lines of this beautiful outdoor attrac-tion. The church itself is quite a lady, but this outdoor path toward enlightenment is open anytime, with a cool-factor that makes it worth a trip to this very posh neighborhood.

THE STAIRWAYS OF SAN FRANCISCO

Rumor has it that SF has more than 300 quirky outdoor staircases connecting our curving, topographically challenged streets. While some such as the Filbert Steps and the Iron Street Stairs are famous as an attraction in their own rights, exploring these hidden gems is a great way to immerse yourself in the city's most intimate nooks and crannies and to see the underside of neighborhoods you might otherwise miss. To find out more about the location and history of these stairways to heaven, check out Stairway Walks in San Francisco *by Adah Bakalinsky, or visit www.sisterbetty.org/stairways.*

Hyde Street Pier
500 Jefferson Street
(415) 447-5000

Landlubbers can pay $5 to tour the historic vessels that dot this ancient wooden pier, but there's really no need, as a stroll among the ships is totally free.

Mission Creek Marina
On Berry Street between 4th and 7th Streets

Houseboats? In SF? Indeed, matey. Only the saltiest of urbanites dare habituate the murky waters between lattes. This floating neighborhood houses the only houseboats in the city in an area just bustling with redevelopment.

24th and York Street Mini-Park Snake

It's a play structure, a water fountain, and a very hands-on piece of climbable art. Quetzalcoatl, the mythic feathered sea serpent of the Aztecs, comes to life in this neighborhood park as a breathtaking, Gaudí-esque mosaic sculpture that is one of the most underrated public properties in the 415. Go and check it out.

Twin Peaks View

Heaps of SF's high elevations offer excellent views, but a drive up to the very top of Twin Peaks Boulevard is pure brilliant spectacle, day or night.

The Twisty Streets—Lombard and Vermont

Any guidebook will tell you about the ridiculously corkscrewed section of Lombard (at Hyde) in the Marina that's more like a slope than a street. But those in the know prefer the less-trafficked, less-touristy coiled stretch of Vermont (at 20th Street) in the Portrero for a fun, short drive of a different sort. Both are sure to throw your car's brakes.

{ **SEASONAL**
CHEAPSKATES:
STREET FETES AND FREE-FOR-ALLS }

"The mint makes it first, it is
up to you to make it last."

–Evan Esar

In case this book has not made it clear so far, San Francisco is a town that loves to party in the street. Other chapters have mentioned numerous film festivals —and how to get into them for free. We've also covered the myriad outdoor concert events where no ticket is required. But there are plenty more bargains for the socialite penny-pinchers seeking a broad range of activities, and they'd be wise to mark their calendar for these excellent annual events that don't cost nothin' to attend. If you're a big fan of crowds and sunshine—or, depending on the occasion, a fan of fog, men in leather, Jerry Garcia, carnival eats, or floating paper lanterns—then the urgency to celebrate in the "free"dom of the outdoors is an even stronger critical push. Event dates vary from year to year, and this is by no means a comprehensive list, but the following action items for your social calendar will let you party without pay or pity all year long.

JANUARY

Vietnamese Tet Festival

www.vietccsf.org

The Tenderloin comes alight with this street festival of cultural dance and music, so much so that you might, for a moment, forget about the sketchy odors that spur from the neighborhood's streets. Though this seems like an unlikely playground, "Little Saigon" has a lot to offer, including cheap beer and delicious, low-priced *bon mi* and other Vietnamese edible delights. Though this event attracts thousands, it is a smaller, more intimate gathering than many of SF's other street fests.

FEBRUARY

Chinese New Year Festival and Parade

www.chineseparade.com

Chinatown bursts into fireworks throughout the month with a host of cultural events, demonstrations, and even a Miss Chinatown USA pageant. However, the real draw is the massive, glowing, dragon-studded parade that winds and slithers its way around the neighborhood's colorful corners.

MARCH

Anarchist Bookfair

http://sfbookfair.wordpress.com

Duh—it's anarchists! Of course it's free! And your mind will follow suit. If this is your political bag of media and progressive, culturally fringed crowd watching, you will not be disappointed. This annual gathering has been happening for over a decade, bringing together more than fifty published authors, artists, filmmakers, and more.

St. Patrick's Day Parade

www.sfstpatricksdayparade.com

Don your green, but don't plan to spend any. This monstrous celebration of the Irish community is not as huge as some of SF's other parades, but it's always a grand cultural happening and a beer-swilling good time. Behold the beauty of Irish dancing, music, floats, and flag waving.

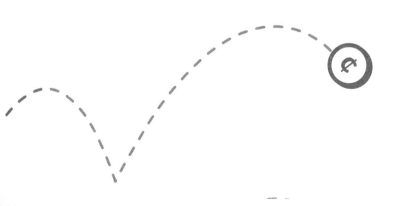

APRIL

Alternative Press Expo
www.comic-con.org/ape

True, this event does yield a ticket price, but it takes many volunteers to make it happen, and if you work it your efforts will save you the $15 admission fee. And it's worth it—this is among the largest gathering of self-published alternative comics, zines, and graphic novels in the country. Not only are the publications cheap, but also this is a great way to support your favorite starving writers and artists.

Cherry Blossom Festival
www.nccbf.org

This springtime celebration wakes up Japantown from its winter slumber. It features boatloads of music and dance performances and a parade, culinary treats, classes and demonstrations, and much more. Many of the events are totally free.

Opening Day on the Bay
www.picya.homestead.com/OpeningDay.html

The Pacific Inter-Club Yacht Association assembles this vast collection of motorized and sailing vessels that gently stream along near the shore for the spectator's pleasure. Simply grab a spot along the water from Crissy Field to Pier 39 and watch these lovely boats—some of which are true antiques—float past and announce the start of the season.

Saint Stupid's Day Parade
www.saintstupid.com

This is not your typical, National Beer Company-sponsored parade. The First Church of the Last Laugh, a loose collective of weirdoes and cultural muckrakers, gathers every April Fool's Day in colorful costumes to toss pennies and socks in front of the Stock Exchange and the Transamerica Building and to otherwise mock the staunch Downtown financial institutions. Don't ask. Just show up and revel in the glory of what happens when street theater meets public statement.

The Sisters of Perpetual Indulgence's Easter Celebration
www.thesisters.org

Gay men in campy nun drag may not be how you celebrated Easter while growing up, but it should become a part of your holiday tradition today. When the weather is cooperative in Dolores Park, kids hunt for colorful eggs, neighbors chill on the lawn, and the annual Hunky Jesus contest winner is crowned—in thorns, of course.

MAY

Carnaval Parade
www.carnavalsf.com

Shimmering bikinis and feathers are the hallmark of this Mission District annual parade, and paired with the incredible music and manageable crowds, this is one you won't want to miss. Brazilian, Caribbean, and Latin American cultures come together to celebrate the pre-Lent holiday—with the common sense to do it this month, instead of in February, where the weather would prohibit the showgirl attire and dampen the desire to shake your rump.

KFOG KaBoom!
www.kfog.com

This local rock 'n' roll radio station features this free outdoor concert and fireworks extravaganza every year to thousands of appreciative "Fogheads." Get there early to stake your spot along the waterfront, as the crowds pack in from all over the Bay Area for the free show.

San Francisco Bay to Breakers
www.ingbaytobreakers.com

This long-standing SF tradition is a race of runners and walkers that traverses the entire width of the city, ending in a huge party and celebration in Golden Gate Park. It costs money to enter the race, but the real treat is watching it, which is gratis citywide. Though the event brings in some real and spirited athletes, the main attraction is the creative costuming, the beer drinking, and those who choose to run the race in the raw.

JUNE

Haight Ashbury Street Fair
www.haightstreetfair.org

The first in the summer series of neighborhood street gatherings, this one has no admission fee but instead features pricey beverages, heaps of vending, and lots of free music and crowd gawking. Note that parking can be a nightmare.

Juneteenth Festival

www.sfjuneteenth.org

This street festival of the Fillmore District is a celebration of the history of African Americans in SF and a preservation of this historic jazz district. Come one, come all for music, food, and special promotions from neighborhood merchants.

North Beach Festival

www.sfnorthbeach.org

Though there's been quite a bit of controversy in recent years about the sales of alcohol during the celebration, this is still one of the more popular neighborhood festivals featuring—you guessed it—free music, vendors galore, a massive crowd, and a showcase of local merchants.

San Francisco Pride Celebration & Parade

www.sfpride.org

Summer in the city just wouldn't be the same without this giant tourist magnet and local holiday. For two days SF is ruled by the power of the rainbow flag, with parties too numerous to mention from the Castro to the Civic Center, and one of the largest annual parades to boot. So much to do, so little time. . . .

JULY

Berkeley Kite Festival

www.highlinekites.com/Berkeley_Kite_Festival

The Berkeley Marina explodes with color in the sky at this annual event suitable to entertain the entire family. Sponsored by a kite shop, enthusiasts will be blown away by the aerial display, flying contests, and lessons for beginners new to the string and tail.

Fillmore Street Jazz Festival

www.fillmorejazzfestival.com

A massive street happening with 300 arts and crafts vendors, heaps of live music, and, of course, free jazz in the street.

Fourth of July Waterfront Festival

www.pier39.com

Nothing says summer like fireworks over the water, and that's what draws the crowds here in droves. This gathering has more of a family-friendly vibe than most, with loads of free, live entertainment, kids' activities, and lovely views all day and all evening.

Japantown Bon Festival

www.sfjapantown.org

This ancient Buddhist festival lives on in Japantown, which, incidentally, is one of only three ethnic neighborhoods of its kind left in the nation. In addition to colorful kimonos and a traditional dance, visitors are treated to the boom of taiko drums, candles floating out to sea, and other historic and cultural practices specific to the season.

Tour de Fat

www.sfbike.org/fat

It's helluva fun on two wheels. The San Francisco Bicycle Coalition adds juice to their chain by doing the following: donning crazy costumes suitable for bike riding and drinking beer. Of course, all cyclists are welcome, the beer is sponsored, and there are live music and stage performances of an edgier stripe.

THE CATCH

This is a free event, but donations are requested.

AUGUST

Jerry Day

www.jerryday.org

Uh-huh. *That* Jerry. Garcia. Of the Grateful Dead. The Bay Area simply cannot get enough of this musical legend, so the devoted gather every year in the Excelsior, the place of his birth, for a mecca of sorts, featuring live music (of course), food, and craft vendors of the hippy persuasion.

Nihonmachi Street Fair

www.nihonmachistreetfair.org

Another summer festival in Japantown, this time featuring the foods and culture of several Asian cultures, including Korea and the Philippines.

SEPTEMBER

Folsom Street Fair
www.folsomstreetfair.com

Consider this a celebration of the leather daddy lifestyle and the place to wear your buttless chaps in public. At least it was. This has become a safe-for-tourists hit parade of what used to be the pride festival for SF's leather community, though now the real experts on the subject celebrate at the Up Your Alley street fest on Dore Alley in July. Still, in addition to all of the usual festival fare, you can be flogged publicly for just a few dollars, and you can stock up on fur-lined restraints in a jiffy.

How Berkeley Can You Be?
www.howberkeleycanyoube.com

The answer is—pretty darn Berkeley. This costume-rich street gathering has it all— music, food, drinks, dance, crafts for sale, nonprofit soapboxes, a kooky parade, and a crowd that is positively and perfectly representative of the 'hood.

San Francisco Zinefest
www.sfzinefest.com

This event caters to those involved with or interested in small, independent, and underground publishing. Though the focus is mostly zines, this two-day happening speaks to anyone involved in DIY print media. Activities include perusing exhibits (free) and zine sales (cheap!) and workshops that encourage knowledge-share in this community (reasonable).

OCTOBER

Castro Street Fair

www.castrostreetfair.org

Yes, another street fair, but this one has dance music and a gayer bend.

Fiesta on the Hill

www.fiestaonthehill.com

Family fun at its finest, this street fair of the Bernal Heights community features a well-kept petting zoo, pony rides, a pumpkin patch, and loads of multiculti family fun. It costs nothing to attend, and all performances are free, but partial proceeds benefit the Bernal Heights Neighborhood Center. Note that no alcohol is served or allowed at this event.

Fleet Week

http://fleetweek.us/fleetweek

Thousands of sailors come into town, the Blue Angels make the sky rumble from above, and regardless of how you feel about the military, the sight of aerial acrobatics will take your breath away. Official celebrations happen at the Marina Green and Pier 39, but anyone with ears will have no choice but to participate in this weekend-long event.

Grace Cathedral's Blessing of the Animals

www.gracecathedral.org/church/new/detail.php?eid=284

As is the tradition in the Catholic Church, this month is the celebration of St. Francis, and that means that dogs, cats, rabbits, and even horses step inside this, one of SF's most stunning and enormous houses of worship, to be blessed for another year.

> **THE CATCH** The service fills up quickly, so get there early if you and Fido actually want to get in.

Halloween in the Castro

www.marchoflight.org

More than a quarter of a million people, most of whom are bedecked in some sort of fabulous costumery, flock to this monstrous annual street fest. Though there have been some increasing concerns about violence associated with the event in recent years, the crowds are always packed shoulder to shoulder, and there's no sign of this SF tradition coming to a close. If you want a blowout street party of live house music, fancy dress, and a crowd looking to keep it going all night, you have found it.

> **THE CATCH** A $3 donation is strongly suggested.

APPENDIX A:

ROMANCE: CHEAP DATES

Money can't buy you love, but you love saving money at all costs. When you're trying to impress your new sweetie, it may not be wise to drop the Cheap Bastard bomb right from the outset. Here are a few low-cost, high-fun dating activities that will make you look like a millionaire in your paramour's eyes:

- Bring a picnic and a warm blanket (for two) to the top of Twin Peaks at twilight, and watch the city light up like a Christmas tree.

- Stick your head into the thrift stores along Valencia Street in the early evening and stroll the nearby murals of Clarion Alley. Afterward, have a cheap dinner at Andalu for Taco Tuesdays or Pakwan, and then venture to Bi-Rite Creamery for an ice-cream cone for dessert.

- Meet Downtown for the First Thursdays art gallery tour. Afterward, go for a walk along the Embarcadero and sip a glass of wine at the Ferry Building's Wine Merchant (tastings are as little as $3). Whisk off your sweetie for a capricious elevator ride at the Hyatt before catching MUNI home.

- Park at the west end of Golden Gate Park and visit the windmills and the surrounding gardens. Split a sundae or get a beer at the Beach Chalet, stopping to admire the murals downstairs along the way. End the afternoon with a walk along the beach across the street.

APPENDIX B:

SAN FRANCISCO RECREATION CENTERS

Always a resource for cheap and low-cost fun and sports, these city-sponsored activity and meeting houses are likely to offer something to cater to your interests. All of these are located in San Francisco, and all are area code 415.

Alice Chalmers Clubhouse, 670 Brunswick; 337-4711

Argonne Clubhouse, Argonne Playground, Eighteenth Avenue; 666-7008

Balboa Park Community Pool, San Jose Avenue; 337-4701

Bernal Heights Rec Center, 500 Moultrie; 695-5007

Boeddeker Park Clubhouse, 295 Eddy; 292-2019

Bowling Green Clubhouse, Golden Gate Park, Stanyan and Great Highway

Cabrillo Clubhouse, Cabrillo Playground, Thirty-eighth Avenue; 666-7010

Cayuga Clubhouse, Cayuga Playground, Cayuga and Naglee; 337-4714

Charlie Sava Community Pool, Carl Larsen Park, Nineteenth Avenue and Wawona; 753-7000

Chinese Rec Center, 1199 Mason; 292-2017

Christopher Clubhouse, George Christopher Playground, 5210 Diamond Heights Boulevard; 695-5000

Coffman Community Pool, John McLaren Park, Visitacion and Hahn; 337-4702

Crocker Amazon Clubhouse, Crocker Amazon Playground, Moscow and Italy; 337-4708

Douglass Clubhouse, Douglass Playground, 26th Street and Douglass; 695-5017

Eureka Valley Rec Center, 100 Collingwood; 831-6810

Excelsior Clubhouse, Excelsior Playground, Russia Avenue and Madrid; 337-4709

Fulton Clubhouse, Fulton Playground, Twenty-seventh Avenue and Fulton; 666-7009

Garfield Square Clubhouse, Garfield Square Community Pool, 26th Street and Harrison; 695-5010

GGP Golf Course Clubhouse, Golden Gate Park, Stanyan and Great Highway; 751-8987

Gilman Clubhouse, Gilman Playground, Gilman Avenue and Griffith; 467-4566

Glen Park Rec Center, Bosworth and O'Shaughnessy; 337-4705

Gleneagles Golf Course Clubhouse, John McLaren Park, Mansell and Visitacion; 587-8987

Golden Gate Park Senior Center, 6101 Fulton near Thirty-seventh Avenue; 666-7015

Grattan Clubhouse, Grattan Playground, 1180 Stanyan; 753-7039

Hamilton Community Pool, Hamilton Playground, Geary and Steiner; 292-2001

Hamilton Rec Center, Hamilton Playground, 1900 Geary Boulevard

Harvey Milk Recreational Arts Building, Duboce Park, 50 Scott; 554-9523

Hayes Valley Rec Center, Hayes Valley Playground, Hayes and Buchanan; 554-9526

Helen Wills Clubhouse, Helen Wills Playground, Broadway and Larkin Streets; 359-1281

Herz Clubhouse, Herz Playground, 1700 Visitacion and Hahn; 337-4705

J. P. Murphy Clubhouse, J. P. Murphy Playground, 1960 Ninth Avenue; 753-7099

Jackson Clubhouse, Jackson Playground, 17th Street and Arkansas; 554-9527

James Rolph Jr. Fieldhouse, James Rolph Jr. Playground, Potrero and Cesar Chavez; 695-5018

Joe DiMaggio Clubhouse, Joe DiMaggio Playground, 651 Lombard; 391-0437

John Muir Schoolyard, 380 Webster; 241-6335

Jose Coronado Clubhouse, Jose Coronado Playground, 21st Street and Folsom; 695-5016

Joseph Lee Rec Center, 1395 Mendell Street; 822-9040

Julius Kahn Clubhouse, Julius Kahn Playground, West Pacific Avenue and Spruce; 292-2004

Junipero Serra Clubhouse, Junipero Serra Playground, 300 Stonecrest Drive; 337-4713

Kezar Pavilion, Golden Gate Park, 755 Stanyan; 753-7032

Laurel Hill Clubhouse, Laurel Hill Playground, Euclid and Collins; 666-7007

Lincoln Park Golf Course Clubhouse, Thirty-fourth Avenue and Clement; 221-9911

Louis Sutter Clubhouse, Louis Sutter Playground, Wayland and Yale; 584-6106

Margaret S. Hayward Clubhouse, Margaret S. Hayward Playground, 1016 Laguna; 292-2018

Martin Luther King Jr. Pool, Bayview Playground, 3rd Street and Armstrong; 822-2807

McCoppin Square Clubhouse, Twenty-fourth Avenue and Taraval

Merced Heights Clubhouse, Byxbee and Shields; 337-4718

Midtown Terrace Clubhouse, Clarendon and Olympia Way; 753-7036

Milton Meyers Rec Center, 200 Middle Point Road; 285-1415

Minnie and Lovie Ward Rec Center, Ocean View Playground, Capitol and Montana; 337-4710

Miraloma Clubhouse, Omar and Sequoia Way; 337-4704

Mission Community Pool and Clubhouse, 19th Street and Linda; 641-2841

Mission Rec Center, 2450 Harrison; 695-5012, 695-5013

Mission Recreation Center, 745 Treat; 695-5014, 695-5015

Moscone Rec Center, 1800 Chestnut; 292-2003

North Beach Swimming Pool, Joe DiMaggio Playground, 651 Lombard; 391-0407

Palega Rec Center, 500 Felton; 468-2875

Parque Ninos Unidos Clubhouse, 23rd Street and Treat; 282-7461

Pine Lake Park Clubhouse, Sloat Boulevard and Vale; 753-7003

Portsmouth Square Clubhouse, Washington and Kearny; 773-1869

Potrero Hill Rec Center, 801 Arkansas; 695-5009

Presidio Heights Clubhouse, Clay and Walnut; 292-2005

Randall Museum, Corona Heights, Roosevelt and Museum Way; 554-9600

Richmond Playground Clubhouse, 149 Eighteenth Avenue; 666-7013

Richmond Rec Center, 251 Eighteenth Avenue; 666-7020

Rochambeau Clubhouse, Twenty-fourth Avenue and Lake; 666-7012

Rossi Community Pool, Angelo J. Rossi Playground, Arguello and Anza; 666-7014

Sandy Tatum Clubhouse, Lake Merced Park, Lake Merced Boulevard; 664-4690

Sharon Arts Studio, Golden Gate Park, Sharon Meadow

Silver Terrace Clubhouse, Thornton and Bayshore; 467-0478

Silver Tree Day Camp, Glen Park, Diamond and Farnum; 337-4717

SOMA Eugene Friend Rec Center, 270 6th Street; 554-9532

South Sunset Clubhouse, Fortieth Avenue and Vicente; 753-7037

St. Mary's Rec Center, Murray and Justin Drive; 695-5006

Sunnyside Clubhouse, Teresita Avenue and Melrose; 337-4720

Sunset Rec Center, 2201 Lawton; 753-7098

Tenderloin Rec Center, 570 Ellis; 753-2761

Upper Noe Rec Center, Day and Sanchez; 695-5011

Visitacion Valley Clubhouse, Visitacion Valley Playground, 251 Leland; 239-2392

Visitacion Valley Community Center Rec Center, 50 Raymond Avenue

Wawona Clubhouse, Sigmund Stern Recreation Grove, Nineteenth Avenue and Sloat Boulevard

West Portal Clubhouse, Ulloa and Lenox; 753-7038

West Sunset Rec Center, 3223 Ortega; 753-7047

Willie Woo Woo Wong Clubhouse, 850 Sacramento; 274-0202

Woh Hei Yuen Rec Center, 922 Jackson; 989-4442

Youngblood Coleman Clubhouse, Mendell and Galvez; 695-5005

APPENDIX C:

BAY AREA COMMUNITY AND CULTURAL CENTERS FOR EVERY CONCEIVABLE NICHE

While not every activity at these gathering places is a free one, many of these houses of neat culture offer some kind of community outreach at low or no cost as a way to spark widespread interest in their own unique style of dance, language, film, food, etc. Check their calendars, get on their mailing lists, and get out there to explore the many multiculti faces that this city has to offer.

African American Art and Culture Complex of San Francisco, 762 Fulton Street, Suite 300; (415) 922-2049; www.aaacc.org

Alliance Française of San Francisco, 1345 Bush Street; (415) 775-7755; www.afsf.com

Arab Cultural and Community Center, 2 Plaza Street; (415) 664-2200; www.arabculturalcenter.org

Asian Pacific Islander Cultural Center, 934 Brannan Street; (415) 864-4120; www.apiculturalcenter.org

Bayview Opera House Ruth Williams Memorial Theatre, 4705 3rd Street; (415) 824-0386; www.bayviewoperahouse.org

CELLspace, 2050 Bryant Street; (415) 648-7562; www.cellspace.org

Chinese Culture Center of San Francisco, 750 Kearny Street, Third Floor; (415) 986-1822; www.c-c-c.org

Croatian American Cultural Center, 60 Onondaga Avenue; (510) 649-0941; www.slavonicweb.org

Goethe-Institut in San Francisco, 530 Bush Street, Second Floor; (415) 263-8760; www.goethe.de/sanfrancisco

Hang Ah Hillside Cultural Center, 883 Sacramento Street; www.hangah-hillside.net

Israel Center, 121 Steuart Street; (415) 512-6203; www.israelcentersf.org

Italian Cultural Institute of San Francisco, 425 Washington Street, Suite 200; (415) 788-7142; www.iicsanfrancisco.esteri.it/IIC_Sanfrancisco

Japanese Cultural and Community Center of Northern California, 1840 Sutter Street, Suite 201; (415) 567-5505; www.jcccnc.org

Jewish Community Center of San Francisco, 3200 California Street; (415) 292-1200; www.jccsf.org

Korean Youth Cultural Center, 4216 Telegraph Avenue, Oakland; (510) 652-4964; www.kycc.net

La Peña Cultural Center, 3105 Shattuck Avenue, Berkeley; (510) 849-2568; www.lapena.org

Mission Cultural Center for Latino Arts, 2868 Mission Street; (415) 821-1155; www.missionculturalcenter.org

Native American Cultural Center, P.O. Box 14408, San Francisco 94114; www.nativecc.com

Northern California Music and Art Culture Center, 3120 Geary Boulevard; (415) 668-5999; www.geocities.com/ncmacc

The Norwegian Club, 1900 Fell Street; (415) 668-8608, (415) 668-1558; www.norwegianclub.org

Pacific Islanders' Cultural Center, 1016 Lincoln Boulevard, #5; (415) 281-0221 (voice messages only); www.pica-org.org (They encourage correspondence via e-mail over telephone.)

Queer Cultural Center, 934 Brannan Street; (415) 864-4124; www.queer culturalcenter.org

Russian Center of San Francisco, 2450 Sutter Street; (415) 921-7631; www .russiancentersf.com

SomArts Cultural Center, 934 Brannan Street; (415) 863-1414; www.somarts.org

United Irish Cultural Center, 2700 Forty-fifth Avenue; (415) 661-2700; www .irishcentersf.org

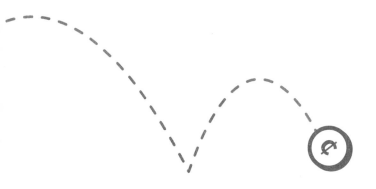

APPENDIX D:

MAILING LISTS AND ADDITIONAL RESOURCES FOR EVERY CHEAP BASTARD

The City Dish, www.sfcitydish.com. Tune in to great specials, two-for-ones, coupons, and downright giveaways in food and drink.

Craigslist.org. For everything—events, goods, services, classes, etc.

FunCheapSF, http://groups.yahoo.com/group/funcheapSF/. Subscribe (for free, of course) to this weekly listserv to find out what free happenings and opportunities await for your social calendar this week. An indispensable resource for any tightwad. Events, food, etc.

96Hours, www.sfgate.com/96hours. Thursday print supplement to the *San Francisco Chronicle;* many free events.

San Francisco Bay Guardian, www.sfbg.com. In print every Wednesday; some free events.

San Francisco Weekly, www.sfweekly.com. In print every Wednesday; some free events.

SF's My Open Bar, http://sf.myopenbar.com. This delivers what it promises for boozehounds who seek someone else to pick up the tab. Events, food.

SFStation.com. Some free events.

Squidlist, www.squidlist.org. Many free events.

www.FecalFace.com. Some free events.

{ INDEX }

ABOUT THE AUTHOR

Karen Solomon is a veteran Bay Area insider and self-described certified Cheap Bastard. She writes about San Francisco culture and consumption for *San Francisco Magazine, San Francisco Chronicle, San Francisco Bay Guardian,* and numerous other local publications. She is also a contributor to *Chow! San Francisco Bay Area: 300 Affordable Places for Great Meals and Good Deals.* She has lived in San Francisco on a shoestring for more than a decade.